Waterholes in the Wilderness

Waterholes in the Wilderness

Encouragement for Dry Thirsty Souls

Kenny Ashley

Grace Peace PUBLISHING

Published by: GracePeace
                                    PUBLISHING

422 East Homestead Avenue
Shelby, NC 28152

Family Picture: by Victorian Rose of Shelby, NC
Artwork for chapters: by Tim Brackett

ISBN: 0-7392-0458-0
Library of Congress Catalog Card Number: 99-96495

Printed in the United States by:
Morris Publishing, 3212 East Highway 30, Kearney, NE 68847
1-800-650-7888

Dedication

*To my precious Bride, Wanda, God's special
gift to me, who always believed
in me even when I didn't
believe in myself.*

Special Thanks....

To my Lord Jesus Christ,
to Whom this book belongs.

To my children, Clay and Kia,
who are the joy, inspiration and pride of my life.

To Nana and Pop, my Mom and Dad,
who modeled the love and faithfulness of Jesus for me.

To MaMa Sanders, my mother-in-law,
who taught me that family is what life is all about.

To the Grace Fellowship Church family,
who graciously allows me to tell them
what Father God tells me.

To Charles and Beth Cabaniss,
who faithfully walked with us through some
of the driest places in the wilderness.

To Jeff and Norma Floyd,
who taught me the freedom of forgiveness.

To Jim and Judy Ebbitt,
faithful friends who love at all times.

To all our prayer warriors,
who held back the enemy while we finished this book.

To Tiffany, Karen, Becky, Amy, and Kelley
for editing above and beyond the call of duty.

Preface

Evangelism has been described as "one beggar telling another beggar where to find bread." I believe that encouragement is simply "one dry thirsty soul telling another dry thirsty soul where to find water.... Living Water."

All true saints of God have suffered from heat exhaustion and dehydration on the journey to the Promised Land. Without His Waterholes of grace, we would all perish. This book is borne out of years of wilderness wandering. Although my journey may have taken me on a different route than yours, the wilderness is still the same. The primary purpose of this book is to encourage you to keep on keeping on. Many times on our journey, we do not think we can take another step. It is at those times that Father God sends us an oasis... not a mirage. It is the real thing. Only the Real Thing can quench the thirst deep within our souls.

I may not know you personally, but we have the same Heavenly Daddy. That makes us brothers and sisters. We will live together forever. In the meantime, we want to fulfill the destiny which Father has given to each of us. In order to do that, we need each other. I simply want to show you where some good, cool waterholes are. I would appreciate your sharing with me some refreshing oases you've found.

I want to warn the scholars and English teachers that this book is written for communication, not for grammatical acuity. Therefore, the stories are written as if we were sitting down for a chat. I know that reading it will be a little one-sided now, but one day we will talk face to face beside the River of Life that filled these waterholes.

Until then, remember that Life is a River... drink it up!

1

Once more Jesus put his hands on the man's eyes. Then his eyes were opened, his sight was restored, and he saw everything clearly.

---Mark 8:25

Remember the story in Mark chapter 8 about the friends who brought the blind man to Jesus? Let me refresh your memory.

They came to Bethsaida, and some people brought a blind man and begged Jesus to touch him. He took the blind man by the hand and led him outside the village. When He had spit on the man's eyes and put His hands on him, Jesus asked, "Do you see anything?"

He looked up and said, "I see people; they look like trees walking around."

Once more Jesus put His hands on the man's eyes. Then his eyes were opened, his sight was restored, and he saw everything clearly (Mark 8:22-25).

I can relate to this story in my own life. I was saved when I was 12 years old. I was saved because I was afraid of going to hell when I died. I believed that God gave you a ticket to heaven when you were saved. You simply folded that ticket and put it in your wallet. When you died and

1

reached the pearly gates, you handed the gatekeeper your ticket and walked right in. In the meantime, you muddled through life on your own, making it the best you could.

For years, I didn't like people. I thought they got me in trouble with God. I wrongly believed the Lord was holding me responsible for everybody's attitude and actions. During that time, people were no different than trees to me. That's the way I saw them. Some were good and fruitful. Others were scraggly and ugly. I really didn't love people except for what they could do for me. I had such a need for approval and appreciation that I used people to meet my own selfish needs. If they could not, or would not, meet my needs, I wrote them off. Oh, I would still be nice to them. I could not bear the thoughts of their rejecting me. But I didn't like them just the same.

With that kind of mind-set and philosophy of life, the ministry became an overwhelming burden. However, I was a wonderful pastor. I told people what they wanted to hear. I was never confrontational if it meant that people might reject me. Everyone loves to be around people who will vote for you especially when you are wrong. Well, I fit that bill to a "T."

My belief system was so faulty; I truly believed my worthiness in life depended upon what people thought about me. My life was consumed with making sure no one disliked me. I did everything in my power to please them. I never disagreed with them even when I knew they were blatantly wrong. I had such an inferiority concept. I thought everyone was better and smarter than I was.

I particularly disliked people who were outspoken and opinionated. Deep down I knew my opinions were as valuable as theirs, but I would never disagree with them. They might not like me if I crossed them. Talk about bondage! There I was in the ministry, called to serve people and despising them in my heart because they did not meet *my* needs.

What I needed was another touch from Jesus. Oh, I had been touched once... enough to be saved, but I still saw people as trees. I saw people's outward behavior. I couldn't see their hearts and their unmet needs that caused them to act that way. I couldn't even see my unmet needs that put me in a prison of defeat and frustration.

Finally, Father had seen enough. He put Wanda and I both through a graduate course of suffering. We were misunderstood, rejected, abused, slandered, and betrayed. All the things I had greatly feared had come upon me. This went on for almost two years. It was the worst two years of my entire life. It was during this time that Jesus touched me again, and I was able to see clearly.

God broke me. Out of my brokenness came light. Stepping out of the darkness, I could finally see. Suddenly, I understood as I had never understood before. God revealed to me that it was not the people I despised, but *my* terrible attitudes which I saw in them. People were like mirrors in which I saw all the things I disliked in myself. Because I hated what I saw, I projected that hate onto them. What I saw repulsed me. I begged God to take it away. And He is doing that. It is an ongoing process.

Allow me to illustrate. When Kia left for college in Alabama, Wanda was depressed to say the least. I felt down as well. With the pressures of pastoring a church in a spiritual war-zone, I did not have the luxury of grieving... or so I thought. I was jealous of Wanda for taking time to grieve.

One day, I yelled at her and said, *"What is the matter with you? Don't you see that I need you? I'm tired of pulling and tugging on people who don't want to trust God. I don't need to pull and tug on you, too! I need some encouragement myself. Snap out of it! Get with the program!"*

Wanda gently said, *"I'm sorry. I just feel real lonely right now."*

BAM! The Holy Spirit hit me right between the eyes. He said, **"Kenny, you are not mad at Wanda. You are mad at yourself. You feel just like Wanda. You are lonely and depressed, too. You are projecting your anger onto her because she's not afraid to grieve. Your 'stinking thinking' keeps telling you that if you grieve, people will think you are not the man of faith you keep asking them to be. Wanda is not a tree. She has unmet needs that are causing her to act this way. Now go and grieve with her. And remember... Jesus wept, too."**

Beloved, do you see people as trees instead of precious treasures made in the image of God? Could it be that you are harsh and critical because you love things and use people for your own unmet needs? Do you need a fresh touch from Jesus today? Oh, how He longs for you to come to Him.

Man looks at the outward appearance, but God looks at the heart. Rest assured that Jesus does not see you as a tree. He was nailed to one so you could see *clearly* how much He really loves You.

2

How precious to me are your thoughts, O God! How vast is the sum of them! Were I to count them, they would outnumber the grains of sand. When I awake, I am still with you.

---Psalm 139:17-18

I didn't sleep at all last night. I tossed and turned. This way and that. My mind kept racing over the prospects of getting this book finished. I kept thinking of all that had to be done. All the things I had to do. Finally, I gave in. I got up around 3 a.m. and wrote the introduction for the book. No sense wasting the time, right?

This morning as I took Snuggles out, I saw my *angel* birds on the patio. I call them *angel* birds because they show up every time I begin to feel frustrated, inadequate, or insecure. They are so tiny. About half the size of a sparrow. Father always knows when to send them.

I watched the two of them hop around, flying and playing with one another. They pecked around the cracks in the patio and ate the bird seed that Wanda had put out for them. Then Father once again reminded me that His eye is on the sparrow (*angel* birds), and I knew He was watching me.

If Father God creates, cares for and maintains *angel* birds who serve no life-changing, eternal purpose, how do I get off thinking that He cannot care for and maintain me... His ultimate creation? On second thought, maybe the *angel* birds do have an eternal purpose. They bring me back in touch with the Source of my strength, my identity, and my destiny. Every time I see them, I am reminded of Father's great love for me. My fears subside. My frustrations are frustrated. My soul rests.

Strange how two little creatures no bigger than a golf ball can reveal Heaven's glory just by hopping around eating bird seed. Makes me wonder what He could do with me if I trusted Him as much as they do. Selah! (Think about that!)

3

Let us fix our eyes on Jesus, the Author and Perfecter of our faith...

—Hebrews 12:2

Awhile back, I was hauled off to the mall... sweet-talked by my Bride. Of all the places in the world I least like to visit, the mall ranks right up there with the dentist's office. But this trip was different.

In the middle of the mall was a small art gallery. I thought the pictures were rather bland and boring. People were standing there staring at these pictures. Then all of a sudden, their eyes would bulge out... their mouths would drop open... and their faces would light up like a light bulb. They would begin to describe what they saw in the pictures... eagles, The Statue of Liberty, dinosaurs, killer whales, space shuttles, etc.

Now mind you, all those pictures were nothing but a maze of dots and glitches. I mean nothing but splotches of colored dots. I thought I was in the Twilight Zone. Either they were crazy, or they were pulling my leg.

Then the sales girl explained that the pictures were three-dimensional and designed by a computer. I was told to gaze into the picture and to focus on my reflection in the glass of the picture frame. I did. Nothing happened. She said, *"Just be still and focus. Keep looking. It will come to you."*

After a few seconds, this marvelous three-dimensional picture just appeared behind all those little dots. It was magnificent! I thought it was the coolest thing I'd ever seen!

I immediately became an expert. I ran around telling everyone how to see the *real* picture. To watch the people's faces the first time they saw it was a reward in itself. Wanda and I must have stood there an hour looking at both the people and the pictures.

I discovered that there was an art to viewing these three-dimensional wonders. First of all, you must look past the surface in order to see the *real* picture. That's why you look at your reflection. Looking at your reflection puts your focus behind the surface where the picture really is.

Secondly, you must be still in order to see it. If people

bump into you, or you are distracted, you must start all over again. Concentration is of the utmost importance.

Thirdly, I found that most people try too hard to see it. You can't conjure up the picture. It just appears when you focus on your reflection. You simply fix your gaze, and suddenly the picture is there!

You know, seeing Jesus is a lot like seeing that 3-D picture. You must be still to see Him, too. *"Be still and know that I am God"* (Psalm 46:10). You cannot look at the surface... the temporal, superficial things of life and see Him. *"So we fix our eyes not on what is seen, but on what is unseen. For what is seen is temporary, but what is unseen is eternal"* (2 Corinthians 4:18).

I noticed, too, that you cannot be looking all around and still see the *real* picture. You must remain focused on one spot. *"Let your eyes look straight ahead, fix your gaze directly before you"* (Proverbs 4:25).

The Word of God is like a mirror. It reflects who we really are. When we gaze into the mirror of His Word, we see ourselves as God sees us. Sometimes we do not like what we see, and we turn away. James 1:23 says, *"Anyone who listens to the Word but does not do what it says is like a man who looks at his face in a mirror and, after looking at himself, goes away and immediately forgets what he looks like."* If we turn away too soon, we'll never see Jesus. Many at the art gallery became frustrated when they didn't like what they saw, or couldn't see. Consequently they never experienced the thrill of seeing the *real* thing.

Those who faithfully stayed at the task, however, were rewarded. They saw what so many only longed to see. That's why James 1:25 says, *"But the man who looks intently into the perfect law that gives freedom, and continues to do this, not forgetting what he has heard,*

but doing it--he will be blessed in what he does." Those are the ones who see Jesus... and the *real* picture.

There is an amazing thing about seeing Jesus and the 3-D picture. Once you see them, you cannot see anything else. The dots... the superficial things of life... they just fade away in the glory and majesty of the *real* thing.

Remember: As you focus upon your reflection in the mirror of His Word, and do something about what you see, suddenly He will appear. He will come to you. No longer will you be able to see yourself. You will see Him alone. And once you've seen Him, you'll see Him everywhere you look.

4

Love suffers long...

—I Corinthians 13:4

Many years ago, I had no concept of God as my Father. Oh, I knew very well that He was Lord... Master... Ruler. My belief system was such that I believed the best I could ever hope for with God was a "Mexican stand-off." If I was perfect and did everything right, then God would not punish me. As for God loving me... Well, I knew myself very well, and I knew God could not love me because I could not even love myself. There was nothing in me to love. Or so I thought.

I also believed that Jesus' death on the cross was not that big of a deal. Father God was God. He knew that He would raise Jesus up from the dead in three days. What kind of sacrifice was that? I would let my child die, too, if I knew in three days I could raise him back to life to be with me forever. I just could not appreciate what the Lord had done for me.

Amazingly, God met me at the point of my need. He's done that many times over the years. This time He met me in a most profound and undeniable way.

One afternoon many years ago when Clay was only four years old, my niece came running into the house crying, *"Clay broke his arm!"* We ran to his side, and sure enough, there was a big bow in that tiny arm between the elbow and the wrist. Both bones in his arm were broken in two. Broke my heart as well.

We taped a magazine on his arm as a splint and rushed to the doctor's office. He was a brave little man. He didn't even whimper until his Mother started crying. Then he started. Not because of the arm, but because his Mother was upset.

While sitting in the doctor's office, Father God paid me a visit. I still remember His voice as if it were today. Here's how the conversation went:

"That's Clay's first broken bone, isn't it?"

"Yes, Lord, it is. I just can't stand the thoughts of Clay suffering like that. They are going to have to set that arm, and I know it's going to hurt. On top of that, it's summer. You know how he loves to swim, and now he's going to miss a whole summer of swimming. It just breaks my heart."

"Kenny, you know that in a few short weeks that arm will be as good as new. You know that you will have him back running around and playing in no time."

10

"Yes, Lord, I know that. But I feel like I'm going to die because he has to go through all this. I would let you break every bone in my body to keep Clay from having to suffer like this."

"Kenny, now you know how I felt when My Son died for you. Yes, I knew I would have him back in three days, but the agony of His suffering, pain and rejection was Mine as well. Maybe even more so. Jesus was My Baby Boy just like Clay is yours. Yes, it was a big deal. And still is. You are my baby boy, too. Why don't you let me hold you awhile until all the pain and fear subsides. We Dads have to stick together, don't we?"

"Yes, Father, we do."

I have never been the same since that day. God began a work in my life that keeps growing day by day. He is such a great Dad. He always knows what I need when I need it.

He's your Dad, too. You know He loves you so very much. He is Love. And Love suffers long. Don't you think He's suffered long enough? Why don't you crawl up in His big old lap right now and let Him hold you awhile. What you are going through is a big deal to Father God... and so are you!

5

Do you not know that in a race all the runners run, but only one gets the prize? Run in such a way as to get the prize.
—I Corinthians 9:24

One day when Kia was still in high school I attended a meeting with her volleyball coach as she laid down the expectations for her athletes. *"You will be on time to practice. You will attend study hall. You will keep up your grades. If you are absent from school, I will call to check on you. Practice is where you earn your position. You will never criticize or condemn a teammate. You will follow the rules if you want to play."*

I thought to myself, *"This is a volleyball team. The coach didn't die for Kia, and yet she has all these expectations from her if she wants to play volleyball. I am a Christian. Christ died for me. I was 'bought with a price,' and I belong to Him now. Nobody holds me nearly as accountable for my Christian walk as Coach Grayson does her volleyball team. Something is wrong here!"*

There are numerous Scriptures that encourage us to be accountable for our actions:

2 Timothy 2:15— **"Study to show thyself approved unto God, a workman that needeth not be ashamed..."**

Proverbs 27:6--- *"Faithful are the wounds of a friend, but the kisses of an enemy are deceitful."* (NKJV)

Ephesians 5:21 says we are to be *"submitting to one another in the fear of God."*

Galatians 6:1--- *"Brothers, if someone is caught in a sin, you who are spiritual restore him gently. But watch yourself, or you also may be tempted."*

There are many other such Scriptures. The point is that we need one another to keep us faithful to our Lord and to His purposes for our lives. We all have times when we do not see things objectively. That's when we need those who love us most to point out the error of our ways, or simply to encourage us to keep the faith and keep on keeping on.

Mutual accountability in the body of Christ is simply a means to an end. It serves to create unity, to generate and build love, to help light the way for one another as we each try to live full, meaningful lives in Christ. Brothers and sisters in Christ are not meant to be hateful judges looking for ways to condemn one another. We are members of a family who only desire the very best for everyone.

Is the family of God not just as important as a volleyball team? We need to practice what we preach so that the world will see that our walk matches our talk. We need each other to make sure we are playing by the rules so that, *"after we have preached to others, we ourselves, should not be disqualified"* (I Corinthians 9:27).

I think it's your serve... keep it between the lines!

6

O taste and see that the Lord is good . . .
                                        ---Psalm 34:8a (KJV)

My Baby Girl got into her car one wintry morning and discovered that her windshield was covered with frost. Of course, she immediately came into the house to inform her Daddy of her dilemma. Naturally, I ran out to scrape the ice from my baby's windshield so that she could see clearly to drive. Being a novice at this driving thing, I worry about her running into things she *can* see, not to mention the things she can't see.

I got the scraper and started scraping the ice away... every single crystal. I was scraping down in the corners, the side mirrors, the headlights... everything glass that had a smidgeon of ice on it. Kia blew the horn and informed me that she wanted to get to school before lunch. I quickly finished scraping the last little bit of ice from the side window and waved as she backed out of the driveway. That's when the Lord began teaching me another lesson about His love and grace.

"Kenny, you did a real good job clearing away that frost so that Kia could see clearly. Right now you have a lot of frost on your windshield, too. There are a lot of

14

things trying to keep you from seeing Me and My love for you... unsettled circumstances, your faulty belief system, busy-ness, prayerlessness, not to mention the devil. Just as you want Kia to be able to see without hindrance, I want you to see clearly so you won't have a wreck in your walk with Me."

"How gracious He will be when you cry for help. As soon as He hears, He will answer you. Although the Lord gives you the bread of adversity and the water of affliction, your teachers will be hidden no more; with your own eyes you will see them. Whether you turn to the right or to the left, your ears will hear a voice behind you, saying, 'This is the way; walk in it'" (Isaiah 30:19-21).

I can see clearly now, Lord. But don't put Your scraper away. My windshield can get frosty again... overnight!

7

Blessed be the God and Father of our Lord Jesus Christ, who hath blessed us with all spiritual blessings in heavenly places in Christ...

---Ephesians 1:3 (KJV)

William Randolph Hearst loved art and would spare no expense to collect artistic treasures that struck his fancy.

One day he heard of a particular painting that he really wanted to acquire for his private gallery. He enlisted an agent to search the world over for this treasure. The agent returned after months of searching to inform Mr. Hearst that the painting had been found. To add to his delight, the painting would cost him nothing. You see, Mr. Hearst already owned the painting. It was found in a crate in the Hearst warehouse along with many other treasures that had never been un-crated.

Often times in our quest for "more," we forget about those treasures we already have. Our health... spouse... children... friends... gentle breezes on a hot day... a wet kiss from your dog when you come home from work... the warmth of a hug... the satisfaction of a job well done... a sound night's sleep... sunsets... full moons... belly laughing... and snuggling with your Sweetie...

Did you notice something about all those treasures? They are all free! Grace gifts from our Father who delights to see His children enjoy the treasures of life for which He paid so high a price. You want to know how to thank Him for all that? Just enjoy them. Take inventory now and then. I think they call it... "counting your blessings." You may have some priceless treasures that you haven't un-crated yet yourself.

With that in mind, let me leave you with some suggestions that will help you enjoy life a little better:

- *Life is short---eat dessert first.*
- *One day is worth two tomorrows.*
- *The easiest way to find something you've lost is to buy a replacement.*
- *Never wrestle with a pig---you both get dirty and the pig likes it.*

- *Out of the mouths of babes come things parents never should have said.*
- *Love is like a kid making a jelly sandwich---you can't spread it without getting some on you!*

Check out the basement of your heart. Where your treasure is there will your heart be also. You may be a lot richer than you think!

8

Be not drunk with wine... but be filled with the Spirit.
---Ephesians 5:18 (KJV)

I took a bath the other night. I don't normally take baths. Real men take showers. I guess I missed the sauna and hot tub we had at the hotel on a recent trip to Toronto. The Lord spoke to me so clearly there. I thought our bathtub might be the next best thing.

I have extremely dry skin. It's inherited from the Ashley side of the family. Whenever I do take a bath, I put baby oil in the water. It works quite well to alleviate the cracked skin and itching. I don't normally stay in there long. For one reason, the tub is too small, or else I'm too big. It's a tub full when I lay down to get my whole body in the water.

I bought Wanda a big car washing sponge for her baths. She loves for me to sponge her back with hot water. It relaxes her. She's almost spoiled, but hey, what are husbands for? I love to play with that sponge. It's fascinating. I picked it up the other night dry and misshapen. I held it under the water and squeezed it. Thousands of air bubbles raced for the surface of the water. I squeezed it again and hundreds of bubbles emerged. Every time I squeezed it, the number of bubbles decreased and the amount of water in the sponge increased.

After many squeezings, no bubbles at all appeared. The sponge was soaked with water. It could not hold another drop. I then picked the sponge out of the water and squeezed it onto my back. I knew then why Wanda was spoiled. It felt wonderful. So wonderful, in fact, that I did it again... and again... and again.

While enjoying my sponge bath, the Lord began to speak. **"Kenny, you are like that sponge... dry and misshapen. I am the oil and the water. The oil of My Holy Spirit keeps you from becoming irritated and itchy. My oil keeps you smooth and soft. It keeps you from becoming dry and hard."**

"I am the Living Water. I refresh you... cleanse you... warm you. Like the sponge, I want to fill every fiber of your being. The air inside the sponge keeps the water and oil out. You, too, are filled with things that keep Me out. Empty things... vain things... fruitless things. That's why I squeeze you. I've been squeezing you for some time now. There's been a lot of things bubbling out of you lately...fear... control...confusion...anger...hurt...pride unforgiveness...discouragement...doubt... selfishness...

ambition... insecurity...bitterness..."

"But take heart. With every squeezing the number of bubbles emerging from you decreases. There is more of Me and less of you. There is coming a day when no matter how hard you are squeezed, I will be the only thing that comes out of you. Then I will take you and squeeze you once again. The Oil of My Holy Spirit and Living Water will pour out of you healing, restoring and saving many dry, thirsty souls. Remember that the next time you feel hard pressed. I'm just soaking you in Me."

I noticed that the more times I filled and emptied the sponge, the more soft and pliable it became, and the quicker it filled with water. I also observed that the only time the sponge was in its proper shape was when it was filled with water. The only time you and I look like we are supposed to look is when we are filled with His Spirit.

The purpose of a sponge is to be squeezed, filled and poured out... over and over again. That is our purpose as well. To be squeezed, filled with the Holy Spirit, and poured out on dry, parched souls.

Has God been squeezing you lately? Have you become dry and irritated? Nerves on edge? Ungrateful and critical when things go against your grain? Hang tough, Beloved. God is trying to squeeze some bubbles out of you to make more room for Him.

Oooo! Doesn't that feel good? Do it again, Lord... do it again!

9

The LORD is my rock, my fortress and my deliverer; my God is my rock, in Whom I take refuge.

---Psalm 18:2

One night when we came home from church, we received a call. It's amazing how quickly your life can change in the space of one phone call. We were informed that my Baby Girl and her boyfriend were lost on South Mountain. Kia, Clay, and some friends had gone to South Mountain for a Sunday afternoon hike.

They were supposed to be back in time for church, but when we arrived home around 8:45 p.m., they had not returned. Immediately, fear jumped to a 10 on my emotional Richter scale. Ghastly thoughts ran through my mind... wreck... serial killer... grizzly bears. Then the phone call... I remembered the words of Job, ***"Behold, the thing I have greatly feared has come upon me"*** (Job 3:25 KJV).

I quickly remembered my recent conversations with the Lord. I remembered how I had given Him everything... my wife ...my children... my ministry... my life... everything... lock, stock, and barrel. I remembered Jesus' conversation with Father in Gethsemane. He had prayed for His cup of suffering to pass if it was Father's will. But I also

20

remembered that one word which I knew had to be wrenched from the depths of His soul... *"Nevertheless."*

As we set a world land speed record on our journey to South Mountain, I uttered that same word to my Lord. I said, *"Lord, you know I love my little girl more than life itself. I would die for her in a heartbeat. Nevertheless, she was Yours before You ever gave her to me. I know that You could never act toward her or me in any way other than perfect love. You settled that issue on the cross. 'Greater love has no one than this, that a man lay down His life for His friends'* (John 15:13). *Lord, I trust You. May Your will be done."*

I cannot explain in earthly terms what happened next. Such a peace as I have never known swept over my soul. His sweet Spirit seemed to whisper in my ear, **"She's okay. By the time you get there, she will be safe and sound."**

Sure enough, when we started up the mountain to the ranger's station, we met some men who were searching for them. They told us that they had been found and were on their way to the ranger's station.

That night, a storm struck... floods of doubt... gusts of fear. *Nevertheless*, our house is standing today, because it is built upon the Rock. That night He hid my soul in the cleft of that Rock along with my little girl.

There's room enough for you, too.

10

"Peace, peace, to those far and near," says the LORD. "And I will heal them."

—Isaiah 57:19

I was not expecting it. Wasn't looking for it. Then all of a sudden... WHAM! The routine of my life was detoured down a road I did not desire to take.

It was silly how it happened. I reached over into the back seat of the car to get the proof of ***The Gracevine*** for the week. I picked it up by the corner and as I brought it over the front seat, the paper slung around and hit me right in the eye. I thought I would die. The pain was intense. My vision blurred. Tears streamed down my cheek. I immediately covered my eye with my hand in an effort to keep out the light. My eye was burning. All kinds of horrible emotions and thoughts flooded my soul. *"How could you be so stupid? Now you will never be able to see again. Your day is ruined. Who will teach Bible Study tonight? You're letting the people down again. Now we have another doctor bill to pay"*... and on and on *ad nauseum.*

I go to the doctor as a last resort, or if I'm about to die. This episode was both. I went to the doctor to get checked out. She came in, introduced herself, looked into my eye

22

and gave me that infamous doctor response... "*Umm... Ugh hmm.*" Bad thoughts and emotions again flooded my soul.

She asked me to lean back in order to put some drops in my eye. It was hurting so bad I would have let her do about anything to me if she could stop the pain. She put these numbing drops in my eye and immediately the pain stopped. It was wonderful.

While sitting there in blissful painlessness, she gave me the bad news. "*The effects of those drops will wear off in about ten minutes. We can't give you anymore numbing drops because your eye won't heal as long as we keep it numb.*"

After that bit of encouragement, she gave me some more drops and ointment that she said would burn like the dickens. She said those drops would heal the eye and keep infection down. She was right... on both counts. It healed and burned like the dickens.

I went back to the office to try to finish my Bible study for the Wednesday evening service. However, the more I looked at the one-eyed monster (my computer), the more my eye hurt. I finally gave in and went home to lie down and keep my eye closed. I found that if I would lie real still and not move my eyes, the pain would decrease, and I could rest. Well, I had to lie there for three days. I didn't even feel like praying. It was an awful feeling.

Finally on Saturday, my vision began to improve and the pain started to subside. I was starting to feel like a human being again. The key to my recovery was following the doctor's orders. The doctor said that the eye would heal if given the proper environment... medicine and rest. It did. Praise the Lord!

While flat on my back all week, I had a lot of time to commune with the Lord. I knew that He would not let this learning opportunity slip by without showing me something good from it. Here's what He revealed to me:

Due to the Fall of man, life in this world is full of danger. Sin, the world, the devil, and our unsurrendered soul are constantly trying to drag us down into the pit of despair and hopelessness. Sometimes traumatic events happen to us due to no fault of our own. They bring much pain, suffering and grief into our lives. We are living and enjoying life and all of sudden... WHAM! Something hits us in the eye of our soul, and our life is dramatically altered.

Whenever a traumatic event invades our life, the pain drives us to try to prevent any further damage. The eyelid of our soul closes tightly to protect it from further invasion. That creates another problem. All our protective devices keep out the things that can restore and heal our wounded soul.

God's children are a stubborn lot. Most of us have to be about to die before we will admit that help is beyond our meager resources. God is the only One Who can heal, fix, restore, and mend a wounded soul. He sometimes allows really painful events to put us on our backs in order to reveal our inadequacies. Though our soul will disagree, that's a really good place to be.

It was only a few minutes from the time that paper hit my eye to the place of surrender for me. The pain was so intense and the fear of losing my sight so overwhelming, I was ready to do anything the doctor said.

It's a shame that we have to let the enemy of our soul inflict so much devastation upon our lives before we are ready to submit to Dr. Jesus. The enemy slashes a gash in the eye of our soul and immediately we try to cover it up to prevent further damage and pain. Then when someone comes with help... with healing truth and grace... we won't take our hand away and allow them access to the wound.

On the contrary, we usually run away from them, don't we?

I remember sleeping far away from Wanda during that time for fear she might roll over and hit my eye. It's instinct to protect a hurting member of our body as well as our soul. That's why we layer over our unmet needs, unhealed hurts, and unresolved issues with strongholds of self-control, self-protectiveness, self-denial, and self-centeredness. Until those layers are stripped away, Dr. Jesus cannot apply the healing ointment of grace to the painful area.

In the meantime, we usually put numbing drops on our wounds to dull the pain. Our soul cries out for numbing drops such as alcohol, drugs, sex, workaholism, perfectionism, eating disorders, soul ties, etc.. But just like the doctor said, the wound won't heal with numbing drops even though the absence of pain feels marvelous. They wear off pretty quickly and the wound only becomes worse.

Finally, by the grace of God, we come to the end of ourselves. We surrender to Dr. Jesus and open our wounded soul to His healing touch. Yes, the Light hurts the eye of our soul as we see how sinful and selfish we have been. The ointment of grace further blurs our vision because we have been looking through soulish eyes for so long. God intended for us to see through the eyes of our spirit. But as we submit to His healing hand, the pain begins to subside and our vision begins to clear. Slowly but surely, hope returns. We begin to understand what Paul was talking about in I Corinthians 13:12... *"Now we see but a poor reflection as in a mirror; then we shall see face to face. Now I know in part; then I shall know fully, even as I am fully known."*

The more we apply His eye salve to our wounded soul, the more of His Light and goodness we will see. It is a

25

process. As we walk according to His Spirit, our path becomes brighter and brighter. We begin to enjoy life rather than endure it. Life gets better and more exciting everyday. ***"The path of the righteous is like the first gleam of dawn, shining ever brighter till the full light of day"*** (Proverbs 4:18).

Okay, Beloved, lean your head back and open your eyes. It's time for another dose of grace! Oh, by the way, if you put your Son-glasses on, the Light won't hurt your eyes!

11

These commandments that I give you today are to be upon your hearts. Impress them on your children. Talk about them when you sit at home and when you walk along the road, when you lie down and when you get up.

—Deuteronomy 6:6-7

Clay is my boy. He's a man now, but he will always be my boy. I'm so proud of him and the man he has become. God has great plans for him. Father God told me one day many years ago that Clay would build the Temple. Let me explain.

Remember how David wanted to build the Temple for God? God told David that Solomon, his boy, would build the Temple. Father said that it blessed His heart that David

26

wanted to build it, but Solomon had the contract.

I started out late on my quest for the heart of Father God. I was a high school teacher and coach for twelve years before I entered full-time ministry. I had a lot of catching up to do. Clay has advantages that I did not have. He's been exposed to spiritual things that took me years to discover. That's why Clay is going to complete the dreams I've had of glorifying Father God in supernatural ways that can only be explained by Him.

With all that destiny and potential in Clay, satan has been scheming for years to knock him off stride. Clay, like most of us, has gone through an "independent" stage on the road to maturity. Beginning with Adam, we all have thought we could make it on our own at some time or another.

After attending college for a while, Clay came home for a break. I was so glad to have him home. I thought it would be like old times when we would sit on the couch, eat popcorn, and watch ball games or golf tournaments on television. It wasn't so.

Clay was struggling. While at college he was faced with questions he couldn't answer. Questions like: *"Why does God let good people go to hell? Why does God let people starve? Why do bad things happen to good people if God loves us so much?"* We've all been faced with those questions, too.

When Clay struggles, he withdraws into his own little world. Chip off the old block. I do, too. Clay would come into the house, get something to eat and retire to his little inner sanctum.

I wanted to love on him, hang out with him, and tell him that he would survive. It hurt so badly to love him that much and to have him shut me out of his life. It wasn't that he didn't love me. He just needed his space.

One day, God asked me, **"Kenny, what do you want from Clay?"**

"Lord, I want Clay to come out of his room, sit down with me, eat popcorn and watch a golf tournament. That's all. I just want to spend time with him."

"What do you want him to *do* for you."

"Nothing, Lord. There is nothing I need Clay to do for me. I just want to be with him... talk to him... joke with him... cut up with him... just be with him."

"Now you know how I feel. You have been *doing* things for me for years. What can you do for Me that I need done? I just want to be with you, too. Come out from behind that closed door called 'ministering in the Name of Jesus' and let's spend some time together. Not time where you ask Me to do things for you, but just time to pal around. What do you say?"

"Okay, Lord. I never knew... On second thought, I guess I did know deep down that was all You ever really wanted."

"Would you pass the popcorn, Father? That was a heckuva shot, wasn't it?"

"It sure was, son... It sure was!"

12

The eternal God is your refuge, and underneath are the everlasting arms.

---Deuteronomy 33:27

As mighty and ferocious looking as eagles appear, they have tender, loving hearts for family. Mama eagles know that eaglets are born to fly in the heavenlies, not to cling to the nest. At just the right time, she will scoop an eaglet onto her shoulders and launch out from the cliff. Higher and higher she will soar until she suddenly dives out from under her baby. That's when he learns what those wings are for.

Some eaglets learn to fly on the first try. If he doesn't, mama will swoop back under him and catch him on her back. Mama eagles are very patient with slow learners... dropping and catching... dropping and catching... until one day, he is soaring like mom.

Alas, eagles have children who are "couch potatoes," too. Mama eagles have lazy, cowardly eaglets that just want to hang around the nest even after the time they should be flying on their own. God didn't make eagles to "snore." He created them to "soar." So, mama will tear up the nest. She will take out all those soft rabbit and squirrel pelts that make the nest so cozy. The eaglet then sits disgruntled on the rock beside the nest. The rock is cold and hard. He doesn't like it very much. Then mama comes along side of him and coaxes him onto her back. Mama's back sure feels better than that old rock. That's when the excitement begins. Mama catches an updraft and leaps off the cliff.

After the eaglet pushes his stomach back down out of his throat, he starts to enjoy the ride. Mama then lifts her nose and begins to climb. That little eaglet's talons sink way down into mama's back. The higher she climbs, the harder he holds on. All of a sudden, mama flips upside down and down comes baby... feathers and all. He falls like a turkey. Just before he hits the ground, mama swoops down and catches him on her back. They then return to the rock.

Next day... launch time again. Only this time that old rock doesn't feel so bad. Baby eaglet is not quite as eager to hop on mom's back, but mama is persistent. It may take several flights, but sooner or later, he learns to spread his wings to steady his fall and catches an updraft. His rate of descent slows, and he begins to glide. He thinks, *"So that's what these feathered appendages are for!"*

God didn't create us to be lazy, cowardly Christians either. Nevertheless, some still want to be petted and pampered when, in fact, God says that we are in a spiritual war for the souls of men and women, boys and girls. Paul told Timothy to **"endure hardness as a good soldier of Jesus Christ"** (2 Timothy 2:3).

God is enlisting us in His Air Force. Hopefully, the times have been few that Christ had to drop you before you spread your wings of faith and allowed the wind of His Spirit to lift you above the circumstances of life. But know this... if you belong to Him, and you are still clinging to the comfort of the nest, the day is coming when that nest will be destroyed, and Jesus will beckon for you to climb onto His back. He will fly so high and so fast that you will be unable to hold on. But not to fear... He will never let you hit the bottom. He will patiently keep dropping and scooping... dropping and scooping... until one day you'll discover the real purpose for your wings.

If it seems like the bottom has fallen out of your life, you need to know that Jesus is always flying nearby... begging... pleading... coaxing you to spread those wings of faith called TRUST and OBEY. He only wants you to become what you were born to be... strong, vibrant children of God "mounting up with wings as eagles."

The ground is coming up fast. Quick! Spread those wings, Sky Warrior!

13

Even the youths shall faint and be weary, and the young men shall utterly fall: But they that wait upon the LORD shall renew their strength; they shall mount up with wings as eagles; they shall run, and not be weary; and they shall walk, and not faint.

---Isaiah 40:30-31 (KJV)

Did you know that eagles go through "mid-life crises" like we do? Yep, that's true. Eagles live anywhere from sixty to one hundred years. There are many parallels in the life of the eagle and the life of the saint of God. God is constantly teaching us about His love, grace and ways. He uses all of His creation as teaching tools.

Take, for example, the middle-aged eagle. The eagle is the most powerful, wonderful, awe-inspiring, and majestic of God's birds. They are fascinating to watch. They are also tremendously strong and powerful. An eagle can grab an animal several times its own weight and fly to great heights and distances with the prey gripped in its mighty talons.

I'm sure there have been times in your life as a saint of God that you have overcome circumstances many times greater than you could bear. With the courage and strength of the Holy Spirit, you took authority over those situations and soared above them. You devoured those morsels of adversity, and they strengthened you. You did, indeed, mount up with wings as eagles as you trusted in the Lord.

There comes a time in a young eagle's life, however, when his strength, tenacity, and zest for life begin to wane. The fire goes out of his eyes and his heart. His beak and talons become brittle and begin to break off. It is a mystery to the eagle.

During this time, the eagle loses sight of his purpose in life. God created him to soar above all other birds. To fly effortlessly into storms. To fear no enemy. But during this time, he comes down to earth. He begins to walk... not fly... in the wilderness.

When eagles experience this stretch of wilderness, you can actually pick them up and hold them. When you look into their eyes, the fire and passion is gone. There is an emptiness and a void. They become very depressed. They do not care whether they live or die.

An interesting thing happens during this time. Old eagles who have survived their own "mid-life crisis" fly over and drop food to these earth-bound sky warriors. Some are so despondent that they ignore the food. They eventually die. Others gather up enough energy to waddle over and eat the manna from the sky.

As they eat, they regain enough strength to recall their true identity. These eagles fly back to the rock upon which they were born. Most seem to remember and return to their rock when re-awakened to their destiny.

Upon returning home, they begin to beat their beak and talons upon the rock until they have no beak or talons at all. It is a most vulnerable... a most scary time for the eagle. At this time, he is totally helpless. He cannot hunt. He cannot fend for himself. He is totally dependent upon the grace and provision of His maker. But slowly and surely, the beak begins to grow back. The talons begin to grow long and strong. His strength returns until one day, He leaps from the rock, catches an updraft and begins to soar once again. It's like being born again.

This event happens only once in the life of an eagle. No one can explain it. It just happens. After this mid-life experience, the eagle is better, wiser, and stronger than ever before. It is a marvelous mystery of God's creation... one through which we learn many things.

I have found in my own experience that when we're young and strong, we feel invincible. We can accomplish almost anything with a lot of hard work and sweat. We can do it! If we get into a bind, we'll seek God out. But for the most part, we think we can handle it.

Then comes a day when the fire and passion is gone. The zealous fire of doing "our thing" has dwindled to a mere flicker. We wonder, *"Why am I here?"* Nothing satisfies us anymore. We meander aimlessly in the wilderness... no direction... no desire... no goal... no sense of destiny.

At this point, many shrivel up and die. Unlike the wilderness eagle, very few fly by with a bite of encouragement and hope. The ones that do fly by are often ignored. Sometimes the saint is so weak that he can't eat enough of it to gain his strength back.

Thank God for persistent eagle saints who keep dropping morsels of grace, love, and hope. Fortunately, some of those eagle saints get involved enough to stick the food into the mouth of the withering saint. In time, the fallen spiritual warrior begins the feel a little stronger... his destiny vision begins to return.

One day, he garners enough strength to return to the Rock of his birth. It is there upon the Rock that his security and strength returns. He realizes his foolishness in thinking that he can make it on his own. He asks the Rock to break his stubborn independent heart.

Dennis Jernigan, one of my favorite Christian singers and song writers, wrote a song that aptly fits our story. The song is called, *Break My Heart*. It says, *"O, break my heart, O God, for it is like a rock so very hard. Jesus, my Rock, come and break my heart, for You're the only One Who can break it apart... O, God, come break my heart."* (Break My Heart, Heartcry Music; words and music by Dennis Jernigan.)

God is so good to break those things in our lives that make us independent of Him. It is only in absolute dependence upon Him that we are truly strong and invincible. And He's the only Rock that can break those things.

After the saint has returned to the Rock of his birth, and the Rock has broken his confidence in self, he mounts up with wings as eagles. He runs and does not become weary. He walks and does not faint.

From that time on, he is never the same. He no longer

takes three steps forward and two steps back. He beholds the Lord. ***"But we all, with open face beholding as in a glass the glory of the Lord, are changed into the same image from glory to glory, even as by the Spirit of the Lord"*** (2 Corinthians 3:18 KJV).

God meant for us to be like the eagle... getting better and stronger every day. He didn't mean for us to "fire and fall back." He meant for us to get better, stronger, and wiser every day as we totally depend upon Him. Jesus becomes sweeter and sweeter the longer we love and serve him. That's God's intention. But, Beloved, that can only happen after the wilderness... after the cross. There can be no crown without the cross. No glory without the grime.

After the cross, Jesus was unshackled from the bonds of earth. His earthly existence was better than ever although He had a wilderness excursion and a cross to bear in order to get to that place. So do we.

Beloved, don't gripe, complain, and fret if you are in the wilderness. It's a normal and vital part of God's plan for you. Thank Him that He has not left you nor forsaken you. Praise Him. It will hasten your exit from the desert.

And if you have been there and made it through, why don't you drop a morsel or two of hope and encouragement in front of a wilderness wanderer today. After all, that's why you mount up with wings, isn't it?

14

Let us fix our eyes on Jesus, the author and perfecter of our faith, who for the joy set before him endured the cross, scorning its shame, and sat down at the right hand of the throne of God. Consider him who endured such opposition from sinful men, so that you will not grow weary and lose heart.

---Heb. 12:2-3

Eagles are without rival as far as birds of prey go. However, they are plagued with nuisances much like we are. We all have annoyances we encounter whenever we are trying to get something done. I call them distractions. Satan is the master distractor. He is constantly trying to get our focus off Jesus. For the eagle, those distractions come in the form of birds and hawks that fly around him and get in his way.

When that happens to the eagle, he will fly directly into the sun. God has given him built in sunglasses. When looking into bright light, the eagle has a film that covers and protects his eyes so that he can look directly into the light. Other birds are not so well equipped. The distractors cannot look into the brightness of the sun, and thus lose sight of the eagle.

We should take heed to the eagle's strategy when distractors come our way. If we would fix our eyes on Jesus, the SON, our enemies would lose sight of us as well. Satan hates the Light. Therefore, Beloved, let us fly directly into the Light. After all, He is a lamp unto our feet and a light unto our path. We will never get off track flying toward the SON.

What's that you say? How do you do that when you have no wings? I beg your pardon. You do have wings. Remember? They are called **trust** and **obey**. Look into the Word. Jesus IS the Word. DO what He says. Praise and thank Him in all things. Think on good and true things. Speak only things that will edify. Sing spiritual songs of praise and worship. The list goes on and on. Every verse you obey is like a thermal updraft lifting you higher and higher.

There's a distractor on your tail constantly hounding you. Spread those wings of yours and head for the Son. The Light will guide you and blind your enemy. So, mount up with wings, Beloved! Now you are flying the Friendly skies!

15

Do you not know that your body is a temple of the Holy Spirit, Who is in you, Whom you have received from God? You are not your own; you were bought at a price. Therefore honor God with your body.

---I Corinthians 6:19-20

A couple of years ago, we bought another Honda. "Hondalina," my '82 Civic was ready for retirement with over 200,000 miles of faithful service. We bought the '93 Civic with Kia in mind knowing that she would turn sixteen that January. We told her that the new Civic would be hers then.

When we told her that, we failed to consider that Kia would have her car at school all day leaving her mom and me with only one car between us. There have been occasions when both Kia's mom and I needed a car. So, I would ask Kia if I could borrow "her" car. She would say, *"Let me think it over, and I'll let you know."*

It suddenly occurred to me that Kia's car was as pure a gift of grace as anything I'd ever seen. I made the payments, paid the insurance, changed the oil, bought new tires, and put gas in that car. It was registered in my name, and I paid the taxes on it. And there I was asking Kia if I could borrow **HER** car!

Then the Lord took that occasion to teach me a lesson... **"Isn't that something? Don't you see? Your life is a pure grace gift, too. I bought you with My Life. I fill you up everyday with mercy and grace. I restore your soul. I heal you when you're sick. Pick you up when you fall. I give you paid-up eternal life insurance and pay dividends... love, joy, peace, et.al...everyday. You are registered in the Lamb's Book of Life in My Name, and I have paid all your debts as well as your sin tax. Then when I ask you to take Me somewhere where I can love people into My Kingdom, you say, 'I'll think it over and let you know.'"**

Talk about your humbling experiences! I feel so bad when I treat His precious grace so carelessly. Why, He even takes care of me and loves me when I get an attitude...

when I don't feel like praying... and when I don't feel like letting Him borrow *my* body.

Lord, forgive me for my ***"contempt for the riches of Your kindness, tolerance and patience, not realizing that it is Your kindness that leads me toward repentance"*** (Romans 2:4).

Now Lord, if you would like to go for a ride, I'm available. Better yet... here's the keys. You drive.

16

Because of the increase of wickedness, the love of most will grow cold, but he who stands firm to the end will be saved.
                                                    ---Matthew 24:12-13

Consider if you will the postage stamp. Its total usefulness consists in its ability to stick to one thing until it gets there. I have not looked lately, but has the word, *commitment*, been deleted from the dictionary? Even postage stamps are useless without commitment, or as I like to call it... *stick-to-it-ivity*. I don't see much of that today.

You may have heard the story of the hen and the pig walking past a country church one day. There was a sign in the yard that said: **Ham & Egg Breakfast Sunday, 7:00 a.m.** The hen said to the pig, *"Sounds good, to me. Why don't we* *drop by and make a contribution for the breakfast?"*

The pig replied, *"It may be just a contribution for you, but for me, it's total commitment!"*

Where have all our heroes gone? What ever happened to our role models? Where are the men and women of courage, character, and commitment who forged ahead against overwhelming opposition to clear the way for others to follow? In the past, there were a few willing to make the sacrifice for the good of others. Today, there are practically none. Why?

In 1945, there were no Blacks in major league baseball. A young Black man of extraordinary talent and intestinal fortitude began to play for the Brooklyn Dodgers. Branch Richey of the Dodgers took the young man aside and gave him the following prophecy: *"It won't be easy. You'll be heckled from the bench. They'll call you every name in the book. The pitchers will throw at your head. They'll make it plain they don't like you, and they'll try to make it so tough that you'll give it all up and quit. But you won't fight back either. You'll have to take everything they dish out and never strike back. Do you have the guts to take it?"* (Hal Butler, *Sports Heroes Who Wouldn't Quit* [New York: Simon & Shuster, Inc., 1973], p.46)

Jackie Robinson did, indeed, have the "guts." Not only did he survive, but he surpassed many of the game's greats. In 1947, he was the National League's Rookie of the Year, and in 1949, the Most Valuable Player. He is now a member of the Hall of Fame. Because Jackie was willing to "take the lick" to open the door of opportunity, many players of all races and ethnic groups are professional athletes today.

There was another young man several hundred years ago that was born in humble beginnings. His parents were slandered in the rumor mill because His mom was pregnant and not officially married. He carried the stigma of being an illegitimate child the rest of His life. He was born in a smelly stable among sheep and cows. He grew up with dirt under His fingernails and splinters in His hands serving as a carpenter's apprentice with His dad. He grew in wisdom and stature and in favor with God and man until He entered the ministry at the age of thirty. Then He was driven into the wilderness by the Holy Spirit to be tempted by the devil for forty days. When He came back in the power of the Spirit, the religious establishment slandered, mocked and tried to kill Him for over three years. He was misunderstood, ridiculed, mocked, mistreated, betrayed, and ultimately crucified although He never did a single thing wrong. While hanging on a cruel cross, even His Heavenly Father turned His face away. But still, He hung there. He never entertained the thought of coming down. It was not the nails that kept Him on the cross. It was love. The cousin of love is commitment.

Jesus could have called it quits and ended His suffering, but He was totally committed to Father's will and to you and me. He blazed the trail. Watchman Nee once said, *"Every suffering Jesus bore ripened into the fruit of obedience. No suffering of any kind was ever able to stir Him to murmuring or fretting."* Jesus never griped and complained much less entertained thoughts of giving up.

How about you? What things in your life are most important to you? Are you willing to die for them? How committed are you? Is there anything that means everything to you?

There are two kinds of people in the world: *trail blazers* and *pathfinders.* Those who take the road less traveled and those who take the broad way. Those who make a difference and those to whom it makes no difference.

41

What are you going to do? Are you going to *chicken out*, or are you going *whole hog*?

17

Put on the full armor of God so that you can take your stand against the devil's schemes.

---Ephesians 6:11

Once upon a time, long, long ago, I played football. After my playing days were over, I coached for several years. Our kids had top of the line pads and equipment. We did everything we could to protect our players from injury. Nevertheless, we still suffered many injuries during the course of the season. I could never imagine sending a player out to play in gym shorts and a T-shirt when everyone else was wearing a full set of protective equipment. It would be suicide to do such a crazy thing.

Just a few days ago, I did something even more crazy than that. I went out to play the game of life in my gym shorts and a T-shirt. I did not take time to put on my protective equipment... the armor of God.

A football player who is not carrying the ball may avoid getting hurt for a few plays, but never a ball carrier. Eleven hostile players with different color jerseys are all zeroed in on the one carrying the ball. Their mission is to hit the ball carrier so hard that he fumbles the ball, or at least impede his progress toward the goal line. Get the picture?

We are on God's team trying to make positive yardage, score points, and win the game. Satan and his demons are doing everything they can to thwart us and to dislodge us from our relationship with Jesus. God knows that we cannot compete efficiently if we do not have the proper protective equipment. Therefore, He has provided for us the whole armor of God. You will find them all mentioned in Ephesians chapter six. Once we have donned our armor, we are ready for the game... the battle... the warfare. God calls it *prayer.* We wear armor so we can pray. Trying to pray without armor is like trying to play football in gym shorts. Crazy... just plain crazy.

Let me explain what the armor does for us. The helmet of salvation protects our mind so that Satan cannot get us off track in our thought life while we pray. Ever been distracted by weird thoughts while you were trying to pray? That's why we need the helmet of salvation.

The breastplate of righteousness covers our heart and vital organs. It keeps the devil from bombarding us with how unworthy we are to talk to the God of the universe. The breastplate of righteousness assures us that we have been made the righteousness of Christ. That's the way God looks at us. Believe it!

The belt of truth covers our bowels. Long ago people believed that our emotions were in our bowels. The KJV of the Bible speaks of "bowels of mercy." The belt of truth filters all of our emotions through the truth of God's Word and weeds out "lying emotions" such as fear, dread, discouragement, and depression. For example, ***God has not given us a spirit of fear, but of love, power, and a***

43

sound mind," (2 Timothy 1:7 KJV). See how it works?

Our feet are shod with shoes of peace. Wherever we go, we go in His peace. No matter what the circumstances, Jesus is with us. And because He is our Peace, we carry His Peace wherever we go and to whomever we meet. Neat, isn't it?

Paul tells us... *"Above all, take up the shield of faith..."* (Ephesians 6:16). The shield of a Roman soldier from whom Paul gleaned this analogy covered the entire body. Many were made of wood and soaked in a substance (spiritually speaking, the Holy Spirit) that would quench the fiery arrows and spears of the enemy. The shield is vital if we are to engage the enemy successfully. When the enemy shoots a fiery dart... deception, temptation, lies, etc... we simply raise our shield of faith and quench it. When the battle heats up, many become discouraged and lay down their shields. That is more disastrous than playing football without a helmet. Keep that shield up, Beloved!

Finally, we have the Sword of the Spirit which is the Word of God. It is both an offensive and defensive weapon. It is the weapon Jesus used against the devil when He was tempted in the wilderness. You must keep your Sword sharp and ready through study, memorization, and meditation. You never know when the enemy will attack, and you will need your Sword. Keep it sheathed in your heart and be ready to draw It at a moment's notice.

Have I convinced you of your need for the WHOLE armor of God? I hope so. Well, what are you waiting for? Let's get dressed. You must be prepared for the day's battle. Ready? Here we go...

Lord Jesus, I am strong in You and the power of Your might. I put on the whole armor of God and do stand against the plans of the devil. In the Name of the Lord Jesus, I bind

Satan and the principalities, the powers, the rulers of the darkness of this world. I bind and cast down spiritual wickedness in high places and render them harmless and ineffective against me and my loved ones. I resist you, devil, in the Name of Jesus, and I stand my ground.

I have the belt of truth buckled around my waist---the truth of God sets me free! I have on the breastplate of righteousness that covers my body, my heart and my vital organs and shows me that I am in right standing with my God! My feet are shod with the preparation of the gospel of peace, and I take those feet and tread on serpents and scorpions, for I have been given authority over all their power. I take the helmet of salvation and cover my head securely, for I have the mind of Christ. The only spirit I will follow is the Spirit of the living God that lives inside me and speaks to me from within.

I take the shield of faith and quench every arrow you throw at me, satan! I take the sword of the Spirit, which is the Word of God, and pierce through your wicked plans, for it is written that all I have to do is submit myself to God, and tell you to flee, and you have to go. Now, GO! in the Name of Jesus.

I place the blood of Jesus over me, my family, my home, my ministry, my place of employment, my bank account, my debts, my car, my possessions---all of which belong to God---and I serve notice that your power is broken, satan, over me and mine, in Jesus' Name.

Thank You, Father. Send people my way today that need a touch from You. In Jesus' Name. AMEN.

18

A friend loves at all times, and a brother is born for adversity... but there is a Friend Who sticks closer than a brother.

---Proverbs 17:17 & 18:24b

Punky Brewster was a theologian. Did you know that? One of her most famous theological platitudes was: *"How can you know if you're happy if you're never, ever sad?"* A similar expression says, *"You can never savor the exhilaration of the mountain top until you've experience the depression of the valley."*

Punky was right. For instance, angels really cannot understand the joy that fills our hearts as God's children because they have never personally experienced the pain and defilement of sin. Because we know the pain of the valley, we also know the joy and exhilaration of the mountaintop.

Over the years I have often wondered why trials seemed to hunt me down. It seemed that I had more than my share. Ever felt that way? Then one day, I ran across a translation of James 1:2 that said we should welcome trials as dear friends. How strange is that? I had always treated my trials as enemies, not friends.

I have also found that pain and His perfect love go hand in hand. When the bottom falls out, you find out who really loves you and who doesn't. The cross was the junction where pain and perfect love most obviously intersected. In spite of His agony, Jesus still loved and forgave us all... every one of us.

During a very tough time in my life, God gave me a poem that expressed the deep longings and questions of my heart. I share it with hopes that your longings and questions may be fulfilled and answered as well.

I used to sit and wonder why trials would search me out...
I'd fuss and fume and rant and rave but mostly I would pout.
My heart would break, my soul would shake til I thought I would die...
The heavens turned from blue to brass as I kept shouting, "WHY?!?"
I guess my Lord gets a lot of that when we hit the rocky road...
We all get weak and want to die as we wilt beneath the load.
That's when the Lord reminds me, "I know the pain and strife...
I know what it means to suffer and die, to even despair of life.
The pain of life lived all alone is more than you can bear...
I hung upon a rugged cross when no one seemed to care.
That's why I send you precious friends who love you like I do...
Who walk with you and cry with you until the trial is through."
There are friends who say, "I love you," when things are going fine...

But the friends that Jesus sends to you will love you all the time.
They don't just love with words alone... they love you with their deeds...
And when they find you in a bind, they run to meet your needs.
They stand and cry beside you when a loved one is called home...
They come to bear your pain and loss and won't leave you alone.
They've learned a blessed secret that most don't understand...
They know that pain and perfect love most times go hand in hand.

19

But we have this treasure in jars of clay to show that this all-surpassing power is from God and not from us.
---2 Corinthians 4:7

In Bangkok, Thailand there is a Buddhist Temple called the Temple of the Golden Buddha. Inside this very small building there stands a solid gold statue of Buddha which stands over 10 feet tall. Its estimated worth is over 200 million dollars.

The history of this statue is fascinating. Back in 1957 a highway was to be built right through the Temple. The monks set about to have their "clay" statue moved. They employed a crane to lift the statue. While being lifted, the clay began to crack. In addition to that, it began to rain. So, they covered it with a tarp.

That evening one of the monks took a flashlight to check on the statue to make sure it was staying dry. As he shined the light on one of the cracks, he noticed there was something glistening inside. He took a hammer and chisel and discovered that the statue was made of solid gold overlaid with clay.

Historians believe that the statue was covered with clay several centuries before in order to protect it from being stolen by the Burmese army that was about to attack Thailand. All the monks who knew the secret were killed, and the statue remained covered in clay until 1957. Interesting, isn't it?

Adam and Eve were "solid gold" at one time. The eternal, sovereign Lord of the universe was their very life. His righteousness and the splendor of His glory emanated from their very beings.

Then one day, an enemy approached them as well. They succumbed to his attack and immediately their treasure was gone. They became mere clay. They lost the precious treasure of God's indwelling presence.

But not to worry. God did something about that. ***"So also, when we were children, we were in slavery under the basic principles of the world. But when the time had fully come, God sent his Son, born of a woman, born under law, to redeem those under law..."***(Galatians 4:3-5).

49

Now, when we thankfully receive the gift of God, Christ Jesus, He becomes our indwelling treasure once again. It is a mystery much like the mystery of the hidden golden statue. *"The mystery that has been kept hidden for ages and generations, but is now disclosed to the saints. To them God has chosen to make known among the Gentiles the glorious riches of this mystery, which is Christ in you, the hope of glory."* (Colossians 1:26-27).

Here's another parallel common to these two mysteries: *The only way the treasure can be revealed is for the clay to crack.* God has a hammer and chisel commonly called trials, irritations, tribulations, aggravations, etc. Jesus longs to live His life through us. In order for that to happen, the clay must go.

The monks thought they had a valuable statue when it was made of clay. What a blessing it was for that highway to run through their temple. Had that road never come through, they would have never known how rich they really were.

Maybe there's a highway that's about to run through your temple destroying everything you value and hold dear. Maybe it is coming in the form of a lost loved one, or a lost job, or a lost relationship, or lost health, or lost financial security, or a lost dream, or whatever.

You need to remember that God is the Head of the Department of Transportation. He is the One who routes the highways of your life. If one is coming through your temple, don't get discouraged and depressed. Keep looking for the real treasure inside. You'll never find it until your clay begins to crack.

Take heart, Beloved. The only people God can use are cracked pots!

20

And let us not grow weary while doing good, for in due season we shall reap if we do not lose heart.

---Galatians 6:9

Two frogs fell into a can of cream, or so it has been told.
The sides of the can were shiny and steep, the cream was deep and cold.
"Oh, what's the use," said number one, "It's plain no help's around.
Good-bye, my friend, good-bye, sad world" and weeping still he drowned.
But number two, of sterner stuff, dog paddled in surprise.
The while he licked his creamy lips and blinked his creamy eyes.
"I'll swim at least a while," he thought, or so it has been said.
It really wouldn't help the world if one more frog were dead.
An hour or more he kicked and swam, not once he stopped to mutter.
Until at last he was out of the can which overflowed with butter. (author unknown)

Makrothumia is not the Greek word for microwave. It is the word for "long-suffering." The word is more descriptive of a crock pot than a microwave. We definitely live in a "microwave age." Even though we like the tasty morsels of the crock pot, we will settle for fast food. That mentality has filtered into the Body of Christ.

We read every book we can get on how to move from "babe in Christ" to spiritual fatherhood in ten easy steps. We go to seminars on how to transform our mini-church into a mega-church overnight. We want it *fast*, and we want it *now*!

We even pray fast. Did you know that you really don't get down to real praying until you have *said* all your prayers. You know what I mean. The prayers you *say* when you think everyone is listening to see how spiritual you are. *"Oh, Father, thank You for Your boundless mercy and goodness. Bless us as we..."* And on and on. When you have emptied your mind of all you can think of to say, the Holy Spirit kicks in, and you really get down to business. But that takes time. Most of us are restless and out the door before we ever get to that point. Prayer is not microwavable!

Prayer requires persistence. Not to overcome God's reluctance to answer, but to overcome Satan's resistance. Prayer is warfare! Don't ever forget that. Real prayer is not for the weak or faint-hearted.

I read somewhere that cheetahs are the fastest animals on earth. They can run as fast as 70 mph. However, they have a small heart and can only run that fast for short periods of time because they tire very quickly. Many people are "cheetah pray-ers." If they can't catch what they are after in a short time, they get tired and quit.

George Muller was no cheetah pray-er. Muller said: *"I have been praying for sixty-three years and eight months for one man's conversion. He is not saved yet, but will be."*

Muller died. As his casket was lowered into the ground, the man for whom Muller had prayed for all those years knelt by an open grave and gave his heart to Christ. Now that is *makrothumia*. That is *stick-to-it-ivity*. That's prevailing prayer. That is churning out the butter!

Ever heard of a guy named Eleazar. He was one of David's mighty men of valor (2 Sam. 23:9-10). He fought against the Philistines for hours against overwhelming odds. He would not give up in spite of incredible fatigue. When the Philistines finally retreated, Eleazar's sword had to be pried from his hand.

What a testimony! When Christ shall come with a shout of acclamation and take me home, I hope he has to pry the Sword of the Spirit from my hand, don't you? God forgive me when I mutter about my lot in life instead of making butter. Did you notice that the circumstances of frog #1 drowned him, while those same circumstances provided the means to lift frog #2 out?

The stronger the winds blow, the higher the eagle flies. We are to mount up with wings as eagles. Blow wind... blow. If the storms of life make me fly higher, let'em rip. God means for us to fly... not flutter. To make butter... not mutter!

Keep churning, Beloved!

21

Jesus Christ is the same yesterday and today and forever.
---Hebrews 13:8

We went back home to South Carolina not long ago to visit with Nana and Pop. We went to the Jockey Lot (the southeast's largest flee market) as usual to pick up some bargains and produce. It's sort of a tradition.

Then, of course, we had to eat lunch at *Little Pigs Barbecue* in Anderson, S.C. Little Pigs has the absolute best barbecue in the world. The quality and quantity you get is unsurpassed. A barbecue plate at *Little Pigs* costs $6.50. There is enough barbecue, slaw and french fries to feed two Kenny Ashley's. Now those of you who know me can only imagine how big that plate is!

Joe, the owner of *Little Pigs*, made a commitment twenty-five years ago that he would serve food rich in quality and quantity at a fair price. He's kept his commitment, and he has endured the test of time. *Little Pigs* looks just like it did when we moved to North Carolina 16 years ago. I like that. It brings back memories. The building is the same. The people who chopped my barbecue 20 years ago chopped it the last time I ate there. Isn't that something?

There is another eating place in Anderson called *Thrasher's*. It's a hot dog place. That's all they sell. Hot dogs. Chips. Soft drinks. When you walk in, they say, *"How many?"* There's no decision to make. Just how many do you want. *Thrasher's* has the best hot dogs in the world. They, too, have stood the test of time. They are still located on an old side street in a little hole in the wall. Their business is selling the best hot dogs in the world. They don't get sidetracked.

In Pelzer, S.C., two miles from my home town, there is *Roddy's*. They sell the biggest hunks of fried fish you ever did see. Wanda and I used to go pick up a couple of plates of fish and grease and take back to our little apartment almost thirty years ago when we were first married.

We passed by there recently, and the memories came flooding back. Those were good old times when we were young and foolish. I remember our rent going up from $85 to $95 a month. We thought we would never make ends meet. My, how times have changed! But *Roddy's* is still the same. Still serving those big old hunks of fish and still not charging for the extra cholesterol. It burned down not long ago. Bless my soul if they didn't build it back exactly the way it was. I like that!

We also went back to the old Pelzer gym where Wanda and I both played basketball. It hasn't changed a bit... except they took the pool tables out. Lots of memories in that old building. Many friends made. Lots of good feelings. My nephew played ball where I used to play. Tradition. Passing the torch. Makes you feel warm and secure. Solid.

There were other buildings that we passed that were not so timeless. One restaurant we used to love is now an insurance office. How bad is that? Replacing a restaurant with an insurance office! It's enough to make you lose your appetite. Well, maybe not that bad.

Then there's my Dad. I have never heard another person speak badly of my Dad in all of my fifty years. He has been a rock like no other I have ever known. He is the consummate servant. He lives to serve. He truly likes people. And people truly like him. Every time you see him, he is the same. He's like *Little Pigs*, *Thrasher's*, and *Roddy's* all rolled into one. He comes closer than anyone I've ever known to loving me just the way I am. He is more of a "God with skin on" than anybody I know.

The older I get, the more thankful I am for the changeless things in my life. Like my favorite eating places, my Dad, and my Jesus. Jesus is, indeed, the same yesterday, today and forever.

I believe that joy, happiness and success are found in single-mindedness of purpose. It is simply finding the **one thing** God desires for you and sticking to it.

Jesus told the rich young ruler that there was **one thing** that he lacked. He lacked total trust in God. Jesus told Martha that only **one thing** was needed, and that Mary had found it. The blind man said, *"**One thing** I know. I was blind but now I see!"* Paul said, *"**One thing** I do: Forgetting those things which are behind, and reaching forth to those things that are ahead, I press toward the mark for the prize of the high calling of God in Christ Jesus."* Peter said, *"But do not forget this **one thing**, dear friends: With the Lord a day is like a thousand years, and a thousand years are like a day."*

Jesus, Himself, made a commitment to **one thing** and stuck to it. ***Jesus gave them this answer: "I tell you the truth, the Son can do nothing by Himself; He can do only what He sees His Father doing, because whatever the Father does the Son also does. By myself I can do*** *nothing; I judge only as I hear, and My judgment is just, for I seek not to please Myself but Him who sent Me.* (John 5:19,30).

Ever wonder why children never seem to worry? It's because their lives are filled with *"one things."* Whatever they are doing at a particular time, that *one thing* consumes all their attention. The word, "worry", means *"to divide the mind."* We only worry when our minds are occupied with so many different things. If we would ever become like little children, we would cease to worry.

What's that you say? How do you do that? You simply focus on the *one thing* that the Lord lays before you minute by minute.

For *Little Pigs*... it's barbecue. For *Thrasher's*... it's hot dogs. For *Roddy's*... it's good old greasy fish. For the Pelzer gym... it's giving kids a place to play and grow up in a healthy environment. For Dad... it's serving whoever needs him. For Jesus... it's whatever Father desires. For you...

Oh yeah... *one last thing*. Jesus wants you to know that you are the *one thing* He died for and that He is dying to love you. There's *one thing* you need to do... let Him!

22

The Lord hath made all things for Himself: yea, even the wicked for the day of evil.

—Proverbs 16:4 (KJV)

Once upon a time, there was a poor Christian lady who had been abandoned by her derelict husband leaving her to raise three small children in a run-down tenement house in a large city. She had no job... no visible means of support. Nevertheless, she trusted the Lord with all of her heart.

Finally, the food ran out. They were cold and hungry. She had tried day after day to find a job but to no avail. Every night she would read her Bible and pray to her Father in Heaven to be her provider and protector. The walls were paper thin, and the old atheist landlord would belittle her faith and yell at her to shut up. He hated people as well as God. Her continual praying drove him crazy. So he decided to teach her a lesson.

One day while she was out trying to find a job, the landlord went out and bought a sack of groceries and put it on her kitchen table. He had heard her praying to God for food. He was going to prove to her that God did not do such things. When the beleaguered saint came home and found the groceries on the kitchen table, she pitched a hallelujah fit! She started praising God to high heaven. *"Praise the Lord! Hallelujah! God is faithful! He is my Provider! Bless the Lord!"*

About that time, the old landlord burst through the door and proclaimed, *"God didn't provide those groceries for you. There's no such thing as God. I put those groceries there. Your faith is a farce!"*

The dear lady stopped and quietly said, *"I beg to differ, Sir. You see, God did provide those groceries... even if He did have to use the devil as the delivery boy!"*

God is good, is He not? He is so much in control... so sovereign. He even uses the wicked to glorify His Name and accomplish His purposes. Vance Havner used to say, *"When God gets ready to plow a big field, He makes the devil pull the plow."*

God keeps the devil around to do the sanctifying work in His children. Jeff Floyd says that when the devil condemns him of how his attitude and actions are not measuring up to Christian standards, he thanks the devil for the reminder. He then surrenders that thing to the Lord. If we do that, there is one less button the devil has to push and use to destroy us. Either we get rid of the things that satan uses to destroy us, or else he will use them to accuse, condemn, and afflict us.

Beloved, everyday God sends to us golden chariots with red velvet interiors to carry us to heights of joy, peace, and intimacy with Him. But there's a problem. They don't look like golden chariots. They come disguised as obnoxious people, rebellious family members, trying circumstances, trials, and tribulations. They are not very inviting. As a matter of fact, we usually run away and hide from them. But you see, those are the things that Father uses to strip our unsurrendered souls of all the strongholds, wrong thinking patterns, wrong behaviors, and protective layers that hide our unmet needs, unhealed hurts and unresolved issues. Once those binders are loosed from our souls, we mount up with wings as eagles. We soar to heights unknown. That's why James tells us to rejoice when we face trials and tribulation. God is up to something good in our lives. Freedom. Joy. Peace. Love. Intimacy.

Beloved, don't reject the next chariot that shows up on your doorstep. See past that ugly exterior and climb aboard. Thank Father for the ride. Then sit back and leave the driving to Him.

23

Give all your worries to Him, because He cares about you.
                                                    ---I Peter 5:7

I love to sit out under my big oak tree. It's where I meet with Father just to chat. The sound of the birds fill the crisp morning air. Tiny new green leaves sprout from bare limbs giving rise to the hope that spring is right around the corner.

I love springtime. It's a time of freshness, renewal, new beginnings, starting over. This past spring was real special for me. God "sprung" up so big. No, God didn't change, but my perception of Him certainly did.

Father has opened my eyes to see that He does SO love the world... the whole world... red and yellow... black and white... ALL are precious in His sight. He is so awesome, mighty, and great. I have come to realize that since He is so great, it is foolish for me to fret and worry about the small stuff. God has reminded me over and over that it's all small stuff to Him.

I used to worry about everything. I even worried because I didn't have anything to worry about. I felt responsible for the whole world. I thought God needed me to straighten everyone out and keep them on the right track. I even felt responsible for the choices people made. Then like the light of dawn, God revealed Himself to me. He told me gently and lovingly that He could handle all that. He was God. I was not. He never needed an *"associate God."* Like the squirrels and the birds which have no apparent purpose for being, I was not created to just serve God. He created me to love me, and for me to love Him back. Period. He likes me. He likes having me around... kind of like the squirrels and the birds.

All of my life I have been like the young man with a huge pack on his back plodding along the road of life all burdened down and heavy-ladened. The story goes that a kind farmer stopped his horse and buggy one day and offered the young man a ride. The young man reluctantly accepted the farmer's offer and climbed up on the front seat. After a few minutes of small talk, the farmer said, *"Young man, why don't you take that load off, throw it in the back of the buggy and relax."*

The young man replied, *"Oh, no Sir. I couldn't do that. I am much obliged to you for picking me up. I couldn't possibly ask you to carry my pack as well."*

Stupid, you say? You're right, but I lived like that

young man for years. I thought it was too gracious of Jesus to save a wretch like me. I would never entertain the thought of casting my burdens upon Him. It never occurred to me that Jesus died for that very reason... to take my burdens away... the burden of sin and guilt and misplaced responsibility. He commands me to *"cast my cares upon Him because He cares for me"* (I Peter 5:7).

Recently, I got rid of my back pack. I took Him at His Word. And oh, the joy! I now know how Christian felt in <u>*Pilgrim's Progress*</u> when he came to Calvary and his pack fell into the empty tomb. Joy inexplicable and full of glory!

Have you noticed that the leaves are a lot brighter and greener this year? The birds sing so much sweeter. The squirrels are having so much more fun. The air smells fresher and sweeter. People are so much nicer. My family is so much more precious to me. My Bride is more beautiful than ever and my kids are just plain wonderful. Have you noticed a difference lately, or is it just me? Or maybe you can't see because that pack on *your* back has your nose in the dirt.

Well, I've got news for you! There is a dumping place for burdensome back packs. It's called Calvary. How do you get there? Just look for the big hill with the Cross on top. You can't miss it. Near the Cross is an empty tomb. Throw your pack in there. That's why it's empty!

24

And we know that all things work together for good to them that love God; to them who are the called according to His purpose.

---Romans 8:28 (KJV)

How many times have we quoted that verse? Hundreds? Thousands? Familiarity often times breeds contempt. We may quote this verse much like the Lord's Prayer. When we just mumble the words out of familiarity, we lose sight of the sweetness and power of their truth.

The Lord gently reminded me not too long ago that His Word is alive and fresh, although ageless. The key that unlocks our prison doors and leads us out of the wilderness is called *promise*. What a great promise is Romans 8:28. If we just *knew* that all things did, indeed, work together for good to us who love God, what a difference it would make.

I recently made a commitment to the Lord that I was going to start thanking Him for everything (I Thessalonians 5:18) and stop complaining. Philippians 2:14 says, ***"do all things without murmuring and disputing."*** After confessing that I had been doing some heavy-duty murmuring, I made a commitment to start looking for the *good* in all my circumstances.

It is easy to see the good in things when they are going your way. It's a different story when things go sour. God was gracious enough to provide for me some circumstances in which to test my brand new commitment. A day later, the compressor blew up in our heat pump. The fumes killed some of our tomato vines. We wilted in the heat for three days. I kept telling myself that God was about to show me some good. He did. The man who came to fix the heat pump was a good man who had been divorced for eighteen years and lived alone. God gave us an opportunity to share our common faith and to encourage one another.

A couple of days later, I was eating my lunch in the office (popcorn and grapefruit juice) when I noticed that one half of a molar was gone... along with the popcorn. Do you see how good God is? I could have broken that tooth with the first bite, but He let me eat it all first. Bless the Lord!

I hate to go to the dentist. I almost started to murmur when the Holy Spirit nudged me and cleared His throat. That's all I needed. I thanked the Lord that I had chipped my tooth off. Then I picked up the phone and cried to my Bride about having to go to the dentist. She consoled me and told me to call Dr. Doug, my dentist. I talked to Felicia, his Bride, and she told me to come to the office right away. I thanked the Lord that Doug could see me so quickly. I didn't even have enough time to get nervous.

While lying in the dental chair, I was reminded about how good God is. I have waited as much as two weeks to have chipped teeth fixed, and there I was in Doug's office less than 30 minutes after the catastrophe. Doug told me that he could not remember the last time he had a break in his schedule like that. He said the Lord worked it out that way. Thank You, Lord, for using chipped teeth to affirm Romans 8:28 to me.

That same afternoon, the fan on my car air-conditioner quit working. This time, however, I asked, *"Lord, what are you up to this time?"* My answer would come the next morning.

I decided on my way to work that I would drop by my regular mechanic's to see if he could check out my fan. The Holy Spirit checked me. He prompted me to visit the owner of a radiator shop who is a dear friend of mine. When I got there, I found out that my friend, Harvey, needed a little boost. His only son was leaving for college in a couple of weeks. I knew all about that heartache. Been there...done that. We were able to cry on each other's shoulders and pump each other up. How precious You are, Lord Jesus!

I thank Him for refreshing an old verse of Scripture and making it new and alive to me again. He is good at that... making old stuff new. Maybe you could use a little refreshing and renewing yourself. Why not take a minute and thank Him right now for where He has you. Jesus knows some stuff. If you start thanking Him for your circumstances, it won't be long before you'll start *knowing* some stuff, too!

25

Great peace have they that love Thy law, and nothing shall offend them.

---Psalm 119:165 (KJV)

Ever had your feelings hurt? Dumb question, huh? We all have been betrayed, abused and rejected by someone we loved, trusted and had high expectations for. Being hurt is an occupational hazard of life. We will never be able to make it through life unscathed. Father God knows that. That's why He made provision for us when we hurt... just as He always does because He loves us so much.

Let's look at the provision. ***"Great peace have they that love Thy law, and nothing shall offend them"*** (Psalm 119:165). Do you see that? NOTHING shall offend them, or hurt their feelings. Wow! What a promise! Do you see the prerequisite? We must love the Law of God... the Word of God. If we love the Word, nothing shall offend us.

Now, Who is the Word of God? ***"In the beginning was the Word, and the Word was with God, and the Word was God"*** (John 1:1). The Word is Jesus. With that in mind, let's take a math lesson. Remember the transitive rule in algebra? If $A = B$, and $B = C$, then $A = C$. My point? Simply this: If the Law is the Word, and the Word is Jesus, then we can say, ***"Great peace have they that love JESUS, and nothing shall offend them."*** Jesus said, ***"If you love Me, keep My commandments"*** (John 14:15).

What does Jesus command us to do when we get hurt? ***"Let us therefore come boldly to the throne of grace, that we may obtain mercy and grace to help in time of need"*** (Hebrews 4:16). God tells us to run jump in His lap whenever we get hurt, and He will take care of it. He will love us, give us grace to heal the hurt, and mercy to forgive the one who hurt us. If we do not obey Him, then the hurt will fall down into that seed-bed of injustice and a root of bitterness will spring up defiling us... and many others as well.

I'm going to be blunt here. It is not a sin to get hurt; however, it is a sin to remain hurt. God has made provision for us. If we refuse to come to Father God and let Him heal us, we are disobedient. The outward evidence of love is obedience. If we love Jesus, we will obey Him. If we say we love Him and do not obey Him, we lie. Love and obedience are inextricably linked together.

Listen, Beloved, satan wants to kill you, steal your life, and destroy you. We defeat him when we obey God. ***"Submit yourself to the Lord, resist the devil, and he will flee"*** (James 4:7). Whenever we get hurt, we have only seconds to choose the path we take. If we do not obey God right then, that root of bitterness will begin to grow immediately.

That is why many relationships have been shipwrecked. We hold on to our right to be hurt. Beloved, we don't have any rights. We gave them all to Jesus when we gave our hearts to Him. We do, however, have responsibilities. We have a responsibility to obey Him. Jesus said, **"Why do you call Me, 'Lord, Lord', and do not do what I say?"** (Luke 6:46).

Have you been hurt? Are you bitter? Have you lost your joy? Your peace? Be honest. If you will be honest with God, He will be honest with you. He loves you very much. Would you come to Him today and let Him take away the pain in your heart? He is a wonderful Father Who hurts when you hurt. Just come sit on His lap and tell Him just how you feel. It's time both of you stopped hurting.

26

Trust in the Lord with all your heart and lean not on your own understanding; in all your ways acknowledge Him, and He will direct your paths.

---Proverbs 3:5-6 (NKJV)

Suppose you were a medical doctor. A patient comes in to your office and relates his symptoms. You examine him and diagnose his problem. You then prescribe medication and treatment and instruct him to return for another visit in a week. Upon his return, you inquire about his condition. He tells you that he feels worse than ever. You are astounded.

"Did you take the medication I prescribed?" you ask.

"Well, I took the pink stuff because it didn't taste too

bad, but those big yellow horse pills were the pits. I didn't take them. They tasted awful," he replies.

"Did you cut back on your fatty foods and begin to walk everyday?" you inquire.

"Well, Doc, you know how that fat-free junk tastes. You might as well eat cardboard. And walk? Everyday? Have you seen my schedule? Now, Doc, can you fix me up or not? I'm not feeling much better here. If you can't do the job, maybe I need to find someone who can."

I imagine that you would respond in much the same manner as would I. I would tell him in no uncertain terms that he better run out of my office before he needed surgery for a broken nose. How audacious! Would you treat a patient who would not do what you prescribed for him... especially if he accused you of not making him well? That's what I thought.

A patient must do 2 things when seeking a doctor's assistance: *trust* and *obey*. If you cannot trust your doctor, find one whom you can trust. If you trust him, you must do what he tells you, or you won't get any better.

Doctors are trained and experienced to diagnose physical problems and to prescribe treatment. Most people are not so trained. How stupid it would be to take some of your doctor's advice, and refuse other treatment because you didn't like it, or agree with it. Partial obedience is simply another name for disobedience.

If we apply this analogy to the spiritual realm, it is not difficult to see why the body of Christ is so sick and feeble. Many come to Dr. Jesus feeling sick with sin and discouragement. Jesus diagnoses the problem and asks, *"Will you trust Me? Will you do what I tell you to do?"*

Many immediately respond, *"Yes, Lord. I'm so sick. Anything You say, I will do."*

Then Jesus says, *"Deny yourself. Trust Me. Follow Me. Take up your cross daily. Walk by faith, not by sight. Listen to Me. Obey Me. Let Me be your Life."*

A lot of people bail out right there much like the rich young ruler. When Jesus told him to go and sell all that he owned, he went away exceedingly sorrowful because he had great riches. What a shame. So many think that they know better than the One Who created them. Who else knows us better and cares for us more than the One Who not only made us but died for us as well?

Jesus once asked a man at the pool of Bethesda, *"Do you want to get well?"* He had been paralyzed for 38 years. It seemed like a dumb question, but in reality many people do not want to get well. They would lose a lot of perks if they got well. People don't expect much from sick folks. People take care of the sick and wait on them. If they got well, they would have to go to work, be responsible, and start ministering to others. No, it was not a dumb question.

Neither is the question Jesus is asking us, *"Why do you call Me, 'Lord, Lord,' and do not do what I say?"* Can we not trust and obey a Lord Who not only knows what is best for us, but Who also bore our infirmities... our sins... our sorrows... so that we could be well?

What's your answer? The Doctor is IN! And He's waiting just for YOU!

27

For we also have had the gospel preached to us, just as they did; but the message they heard was of no value to them, because those who heard did not combine it with faith.

---Hebrews 4:2

Why do we have problems? Why is living oftentimes such a struggle? When is the last time you whistled while you worked? Would you say that your life is full of joy? Are you at peace? Are you content with your lot in life? If not, why not?

If these are the questions, then Jesus is the Answer. He is the great "I AM." Whatever we need, Jesus IS the answer, the solution, the provision. He is our ALL-IN-ALL.

If that is true, and He is the Truth, then why do we feel so rotten? Simple. We do not believe in God's system. God's system is based on faith. It never fails. God always says what He means, and He means what He says. Faith is the key that makes God's system operative in our lives.

Some of you may be getting defensive on me right about now. You say that you have faith, but you have no real joy. I say, "Bull feathers!" You have no joy because you have no faith. Jesus said, ***"If you obey My commands, you will remain in My love, just as I have obeyed My Father's***

71

commands and remain in His love. I have told you this so that My joy may be in you and that your joy may be complete" (John 15:10-11).

What is faith? Faith is simply knowing the mind, the thoughts, the commands of God and being obedient. Our joy, or the lack thereof, is directly linked to our obedience. If we obey God, joy will result. Jesus said so. That is God's system. We believe... we trust... we obey and He supplies, produces, and becomes the provision... the solution... the answer.

I met a man some time ago that trusted God's system. Because he trusted God's system, God was more real to him than anyone I know. Earnest Mayley took God seriously. He cut his finger off at work one day and praised God for putting McDonald's napkins in his truck to help stop the bleeding. He said that we should give thanks for all things because all things work together for good to them that love God and are called according to His purpose. Earnest was obedient, and God was faithful. Joy flowed from this man like a river.

But you say, *"I trust God, but I don't **feel** joy, peace, love, etc. "* That is because your starting point is feelings, not Truth. Picture in your mind an old-timey choo-choo train with a steam-engine locomotive, a coal car, and a caboose. Let the engine represent Truth, the fact of God's Word. The train engine must have fuel to make it run. Let the coal car represent Faith. God's train needs Faith for fuel. No fuel... no power. God's engine, His Word, will not work for you if it has no fuel (faith). However, when you pour on the coal (faith), that engine (God's Word) becomes more powerful than a locomotive that not only leaps mountains in a single bound, but moves them completely out of the way!

God's caboose represents our feelings. The caboose

has no power of its own. Without the engine and coal car, it sits helplessly on the track. It moves only when the engine runs, and the engine only runs when we pour on the coal. When we pour faith into God's Word, the caboose (feelings) will follow. Count on it! It's part of God's system. And God's system never fails.

Remember the children's story about the little train that faced the mountain and kept saying, *"I think I can! I think I can!"*? As God's children facing mountains of fear, doubt and confusion, we can surely overcome them because God says, *"I know you can! I know you can!"*

Beloved, it's time to fire up that old locomotive. All aboard! This is one "soul" train you don't want to miss!

28

He tends His flock like a shepherd; He gathers the lambs in His arms and carries them close to His heart...

—Isaiah 40:11

There are times when His Word is good to our souls bringing joy, peace and encouragement. At other times, it seems like we need a little more than His written, or spoken Word. We need the Living Word... the Good Shepherd, Himself, to put His arms around us and just hold us. Nothing else will still the turmoil of doubt and fear that assaults our souls from time to time.

My good friend and prayer partner, Jim Brackett, shared with me a childhood experience of his that has blessed my heart many times during storms of fear and doubt. He recalls going to a relative's home to visit on a Sunday afternoon. This relative had a big black dog that jumped up on everyone that came into the yard. Jim, being a little boy at the time, was scared to death of that big black dog.

When his family pulled up into the yard, everyone got out to go inside... everybody, that is, except Jim. Jim was not about to get out of the car with that monster dog between him and the front porch. His dad got to the steps and noticed Jim was still in the backseat.

His dad said, *"Jim, get out of the car and come on into the house."*

Jim said, *"Not with that dog there."*

His dad tried to encourage him. *"Jim, that dog will not hurt you. Now, come here."*

"No, sir! If you want me in the house, you'll have to come carry me!"

Jim's dad finally came back to the car and carried his son into the house. Jim said that he felt so secure in his dad's arms. He knew that it didn't matter how big and bad that old dog was as long as his dad held him.

There are times in my life when I hear God's Word so clear in my mind... *"Be strong and courageous. I will never leave you nor forsake you. Greater is He that is in you than he that is in the world."* I know all that in my mind, but my heart isn't listening. At those times, I need more than His Word. I need Him... Jesus... the Good Shepherd to come gather ME up in His arms and carry me close to His heart.

He's not reluctant to do that, you know. As a matter of fact, He longs to hold us close to His heart. He made us so He could love us, but sometimes we like sheep go astray. That's when the big black dogs of the enemy drive us into the back seat of life where we lock the doors and tremble with fear. That's when we need more than reassuring words. We need the strong arms of the Good Shepherd to lift us up out of reach of the big black dogs.

He knows His children are frightened sometimes... maybe a lot of the time. That's why Jesus said, ***"'Let the little children come to me, and do not hinder them, for the kingdom of God belongs to such as these'... And He took the children in His arms, put His hands on them and blessed them"*** (Mark 10:14 & 16).

Remember, Beloved, no matter how old you are, you will always be a child in His eyes.

29

A bruised reed He will not break, and a smoldering wick He will not snuff out.

---Matthew 12:20

I never ceased to be amazed at the number of ways God speaks to us. I see Him say, **"I love you"** through a robin's eggs, sunsets, purple-flowered weeds, hugs from children, a snuggle with your Bride, and a cool breeze upon a sweaty brow.

By His grace, God has opened my eyes to His goodness. Now, I can see Him jumping up and down trying desperately to get His children's attention. He is waving His hands and shouting, **"I LOVE YOU!"** And still many are blind to that fact. I hear people demand to know why God allows suffering, and yet they walk by His innumerable blessings everyday oblivious to His love, mercy and grace!

Nevertheless, God loves the spiritually blind as well. He gave me a glimpse of His compassion one night not too long ago. I had gone to visit a friend when she directed my attention to the shrubbery beside the front porch. There in the bushes, cowering in a frightened heap just barely out of sight, was a tiny black and brown puppy. After much "sweet talking" and coaxing, the puppy finally mustered up the courage to inch forward enough to *sniff* my outstretched hand. The sniff gave her enough assurance to allow me to softly pat her nose... then her head... until finally I was stroking her trembling body. My friend informed me that the puppy just showed up one day starving and trembling behind the hedges. Obviously, the dog had been the victim of abuse and ill-treatment... not unlike many people we pass on the street everyday.

All of us have experienced the pain of mistreatment... some more than others. For some, it was an alcoholic father, or a mother we could not please, or a spouse who walked away, or a defiant teenager who ran away from home, or a relationship that turned sour and left a deep gash in the heart. I can imagine that little puppy had seen her share of heartache. I am sure there were hands extended to her in love which suddenly turned without warning into instruments of pain and rejection.

The healing of a wounded spirit takes time. That is why Isaiah said of Jesus... ***"A bruised reed He will not break, and a smoldering wick He will not snuff out"*** (Matthew 12:20). The spirit of that little puppy was broken but still dangling... at the point of dying yet flickering. A hand extended in compassion fanned the hope of love and acceptance in the heart of that little puppy. The warmth of hope overcame the chill of fear until inch by inch, courage overcame fright, and faith swallowed up hopelessness.

Aren't you glad that Jesus always has His hand of mercy and grace extended toward us? Won't you let His strength and courage rise up against the fear in your soul at least enough to *sniff* His hand? Do you smell the fragrance of His grace? Inch forward a little more and let Him soothe the longing in your heart for His unconditional love and acceptance. Patiently, He waits for you to allow Him to stroke your tortured soul with grace and peace. Relax... enjoy... rest in His love.

And when you have savored the fulness of the Master's love, maybe you will allow His hand to slip inside of yours to reach out to another who may be cowering anxiously in a weed-bed of life. Be patient... keep the faith... know that the Promised Land is only a *sniff* away!

30

"Do not lose heart when He rebukes you, because the Lord disciplines those He loves..."
---Hebrews 12:5-6

God speaks to His children in the strangest ways. Just the other day, the Lord used a little white fuzz-ball of energy named Snuggles, our new Samoyed puppy, to teach me a valuable lesson about His love and grace.

During her obedience school days, I secured a dog training book by a leading trainer. I was shocked by his techniques. However shocked I might have been, I began using them on Snuggles. The purpose of the first lesson was to train her to focus full attention on her master. The technique was simple. A choker collar (one that tightens as pressure is applied) was placed around her neck and connected to 20 feet of rope. Several spots were selected throughout the yard. Snuggles and I were to walk to each spot and remain there for several minutes. No communication was to take place between us... just walk and stop.

Snuggles did quiet well the first few stops. Then a visitor came out of our house and started for her car. Snuggles, loving people as she does, lit out for the lady in hopes of getting a love pat or two. I just stood there. Snuggles kept running... right out of rope. BAM! She cut a flip and landed right on her back. She got up and looked at me like a calf looks at a new gate. One thing for sure, she kept her eyes on me from then on. When I walked... she walked. When I stopped... she stopped. She learned a valuable lesson: *When your master has the rope, you better keep your eyes on him.*

While Snuggles was learning in the school of "hard knocks," God took occasion to teach me a thing or two. He said, "**Jordan** (our Cocker Spaniel who was killed 5 weeks earlier) **would still be here if you had loved him enough to train him. But you thought he wouldn't love you if you disciplined him, didn't you? Because you didn't love him enough to make him mind, he met a truck who didn't know he was just playing in the road. When I let you come to the end of your rope, I'm showing how much I really love you. There are people, places and things that are dangerous for you. A sore neck is a small price to pay to keep you from hurting yourself... and others. I love you too much to let you go. Remember... I'll always love you... sore neck and all!"**

31

Jesus answered, "I am the way, the truth, and the life. No one comes to the Father except through Me."

---John 14:6

Snuggles, our Samoyed puppy of fourteen weeks, has walked right into our home and has begun to fill the hole in our hearts left by the death of Jordan, our Cocker Spaniel. God has really used Snuggles as a living object lesson of His relationship to me and my spiritual journey with Him.

As I write this episode, Blackie, the old stray mixed breed living in our carport with her brood of pups, comes barking and snorting out of the carport. She sees Snuggles and me sitting on the sidewalk and saunters over for a little TLC (tender loving care).

Snuggles can't stand sharing *her* attention. So, she commences to jump on Blackie's back and bite her neck and ears. Being four times the size of Snuggles, Blackie is content to put up with the nuisance for a while in exchange for a few love pats. Just the other day, Blackie was not in such a congenial mood. Snuggles bit her ear, and Blackie bit her head. You would have thought that Snuggles would have learned from that experience, but alas, she did not.

Then God said to me, "**Kenny, you're just a puppy like Snuggles. Everything distracts your attention from Me. I have as much difficulty training you as you have training Snuggles. You have learned in your dog training book that you will never be able to teach your dog anything until she pays absolute attention to you, her master, at all times. Can you imagine what would happen to a blind person if his seeing eye dog lost his sense of purpose every time the least distraction caught his eye? You must train Snuggles to always be aware of where you are, and what you're doing all the time. That training is for her benefit even though she doesn't know it."**

"**Losing sight of you can mean death for her. Losing sight of Me can mean the same for you. But more importantly, it can mean spiritual death to those who are watching you. Pay attention... I AM the Way!"**

32

The Lord your God is with you; the Mighty One will save you. He will rejoice over you. You will rest in His love; He will sing and be joyful about you.

---Zephaniah 3:17

One night when I got home from church, I went to the

grocery store to pick up a few things for Clay to eat. Strange thing about that boy... he thinks he has to eat everyday. Snuggles went with me. You mention the "G" word (GO!), and she is out the door and in the front seat of the car blowing the horn. She loves to ride. I love her company.

Inside the store, I remembered that Wanda had seen this commercial on TV about chocolate-covered pretzels. Her mouth waters every time she sees it. I finally found her treasure on the candy aisle. I got excited just thinking about how much she was going to enjoy the treat. I live to make her happy. She is my pride and joy... the apple of my eye. I love her with all my heart.

I made my purchase and headed down the road. Then I heard Him whisper, **"You're excited, aren't you? Can't wait to get home and surprise your Sweetie. It blesses you to do things like that for her, doesn't it?"**

"I get butterflies just thinking about it, Father. I love her so much. You did real good when you gave her to me."

"Do you think you love her more than I do? I made her just for you. I take great delight in doing things for you, too. I'm always looking to bless you. I know the plans I have for you. Plans to prosper and bless you. Plans to give you a future and a hope. I get butterflies, too, thinking about how much you are going to enjoy My blessings made especially for you."

"Father, that's hard for me to imagine. No one has ever loved me like that before. I've had to earn my love all my life. When I didn't measure up, people didn't love me anymore. How can you love me like that when You, most of all, know how far short I've fallen?"

"Look at Snuggles. You love that old dog, don't you? When Jordan died, I sent Snuggles to you to fill up the hole in your heart. She's been a blessing, hasn't she?

Why do you love her? She's just an old dog. She throws up on the floor because she has a weak stomach just like the rest of the family. You have to clean up after her. Get up early and let her out. Why do you love her?"

"I don't know, Father. I just do. She's always glad to see me when I get home. Always greets me at the door. Let's me pet her whenever I want to. Licks my ear when I rub her stomach. She loves me. She accepts me just the way I am all the time... even when I'm in a bad mood. I know she's not good for much. She sheds and pukes. I have to clean up after her. But she's my dog. I just love her."

"There's a lot of parallels between you and Snuggles. You ask Me how I can love you the way I do? I don't need you to do anything for Me. You think I do, but I don't. I didn't create you to do stuff for me. I created you to love Me, and to let me love you. Did you get Snuggles to do some stuff for you? I don't think so. You say you love Snuggles because she's your dog. Well, I love you because you're my boy. I get excited, too, when you come home and spend time with Me... even when you're in a bad mood. I delight in blessing you a lot more than you delight in blessing Snuggles with a bone from Wal-Mart and Wanda with a bag of pretzels. I just love you. You want to know how you can bless Me? Just let Me bless you. Enjoy it!"

Thanks, Father. Will you pass the pretzels, please?

33

"I tell you the truth, whatever you did for one of the least of these brothers of mine, you did for Me."

---Matthew 25:40

She's a nuisance. She is messy. She is constantly being run off from places. Timid doesn't begin to portray her ...cowardly ...fearful ...deathly afraid describes her better. Take a step toward her, and she tucks her tail and runs. Nobody wants anything to do with her. If the truth were known, most people couldn't care less if she was dead.

Our family calls her "Blackie." She's an old stray dog... mostly Labrador Retriever with a little "sooner" in her (as soon be one breed as another). She has been great with child (or puppy) for the last couple of weeks. She's been a nuisance because she's been hungry. Hungry for food and hungry for some love and attention. It's obvious that she's been mistreated. She cowers down whenever anyone reaches out toward her head. Pitiful... alone... nowhere to turn.

We have been leaving some food for her for the last few weeks outside the carport. She sneaks in and eats, and then leaves before someone comes and runs her off. We haven't seen her in about a week.

Last Sunday a blizzard blew into town. We heard Blackie barking in the woods behind the house. She never barks, so we investigated. Piled up under an old fallen tree in the middle of a mud hole were TEN black, one week-old puppies shivering in the cold.

After trying to make some shelter for her family, we took her some food and water. It was strange. She waddled up to us without any sign of fear. It was if she could trust again because kindness had been shown in little bits over a period of time. Then as if the walls fell all at once, she opened up and accepted our love and assistance.

Needless to say, Blackie and her brood came to reside on our carport. I couldn't bear the thoughts of calling the "dog catcher." That would have been a dead end trip for Blackie. So, we made the commitment to see her through this episode in her storm-tossed life. It was costly...a hassle... an inconvenience. But you know, one lick on the hand and one wagging tail more than made up for all the trouble.

I wonder how many people "Blackies" are running around our town. Scared... hurt... over-burdened and under-nourished... starving for the basic needs of life... love, acceptance, respect. It's easy to call the Salvation Army, or give them some canned goods, but are we willing to endure the hassles in order to meet their eternal needs?

Need is simply the prompting of God to come to Him for the supply. When need meets supply, walls fall down and love abounds. What are you waiting for?

34

For the love of Christ constrains us....

—2 Corinthians 5:14

One Wednesday night after prayer service, I took a walk around the block. Snuggles had a fit to go with me. So I leashed her up and off we went. She was a wild woman! She would run over and sniff the bushes. Then she would chase those flying varmints that come out after dark. The sounds of night fascinated her. She would run... stop... perk up her ears... then take off again in search of new discoveries. She was totally absorbed by her environment... that is, everything in her environment but me, her master.

About a quarter of a mile from the house, we heard the clickety click of toenails pounding the road. Blackie couldn't resist the fellowship and hustled to join us. She had no leash, but she didn't need one. Her eyes never left me. When I stopped walking, she stopped. When I walked, she walked. When I ran, she ran. It was as if we were one soul.

I was reminded of Psalm 123:1-2... ***"Unto You I lift up my eyes, O You Who dwell in the heavens. Behold, as the eyes of servants look to the hand of their masters, as the eyes of a maid to the hand of her mistress, so our eyes look to the Lord our God, until He has mercy on us."***

86

That was Blackie. She anticipated every move I made. Oh, that we were so attentive to our Master!

I thought about my own children and how much like Snuggles they were. Yes, they belong to the Master just as Snuggles belongs to me. They know their Dad loves them. They know that their every need will be met. And yet, the excitement of the world is so enticing. Their eyes are so easily diverted from the face and hand of the one who loves them most. It is not a question of love. It's just that there is so much of life yet to be lived... dating... school... sports... proms... college... career... marriage... family. Life in the eyes of children is like Las Vegas to a country boy who's never been off the farm. It is mesmerizing.

It's that same glitter that blinds their eyes to the griefs and sorrows of life. They have yet to discover that life is a mixture of joy and sorrow... victory and defeat... mountaintops and valleys. They don't understand that it's the downside that makes the upside so meaningful and highlights the truly valuable things in life.

Those of us who have been following the Master for years are more like Blackie. She has known the bliss of puppyhood. She's known the sobering responsibility and joy of motherhood. She's felt the pain and rejection that life can dish out. She's experienced it all. Now, the thing that matters most is her Master. Everything else pales in comparison to just being in his presence.

Blackie needs no leash. The love of her Master constrains her... Me, too! How about you?

35

"When Jesus rose early on the first day of the week, He appeared first to Mary Magdalene, out of whom he had driven seven demons."

---Mark 16:9

When Jesus rose from the tomb on that first Easter morning, **"He appeared FIRST to Mary Magdalene out of whom He had cast seven demons."** After reading that verse, I began to ponder the significance of His appearing to Mary Magdalene *first*.

One morning, God gave me a visual aid. When I went out to feed Blackie and her puppies, Blackie jumped up on me, put her paws around my neck, and began licking me in the face. Immediately, the Holy Spirit brought another verse to mind... John 20:17 (KJV)... **"Jesus said to Mary, 'Do not cling to Me, for I have not yet ascended to My Father.'"**

Then it hit me! Mary and Blackie have so much in common. Both were outcastes of society. Both were doomed to die in their particular lifestyles. Both had been abused. Both were hopeless. Both found saviors who took them in and loved them unconditionally. No wonder Mary and Blackie were "clingers." When you find someone who loves you like that you don't ever want to let go of them.

It's interesting to me that John is the only Gospel writer who uses such an illustrative word as "cling." Luke didn't even mention Jesus' conversation with Mary. That's ironic since Luke had a passion for detail. Mark didn't mention the conversation because he leans more toward the actions of Christ rather than His discourses. Matthew comes closest to John's account when he says, "*...they came and held Him by the feet and worshiped Him*" (Matthew 28:9).

Of all the disciples, it was John whose heart was most in tune with our Lord's. John referred to himself as "*the disciple whom the Lord loved.*" John was flabbergasted at the thought of the Son of God loving him. John knew and treasured that love unlike many who followed Jesus. It was John who laid his head on Jesus' bosom at the Last Supper. It was John to whom Jesus entrusted the care of His mother. It was John who first recognized Jesus on the shore following His resurrection.

Jeremiah 29:13 says, "*And you will seek Me and find Me, when you search for Me with all your heart.*" Those who have been radically impacted by His love are always seeking to stay close to Him. They see Him first because they are always looking *to* Him and *for* Him.

If we lose sight of Jesus too easily, maybe we have forgotten where we were when He found us. Mary and Blackie never forgot. "Clingers" have great memories. Maybe we need to sharpen ours.

89

36

Blessed is the man who perseveres under trial, because when he has stood the test, he will receive the crown of life that God has promised to those who love Him.

---James 1:12

I broke down and cut my grass the other day. I didn't want to because it has been so dry. The grass crunches underfoot due to the lack of rain. Although the grass has stopped growing, our weeds are flourishing. Where the grass was parched brown, the weeds stood in stark contrast with their bright green luster. They grew so tall that I was ashamed to let them mock the grass I have so pampered, fertilized and manicured.

As I was mowing, I began to think how Christians ought to be like weeds. We are rejects in this world system. James 2:15-17 aptly states that truth: **"Do not love the world or anything in the world. If anyone loves the world, the love of the Father is not in him. For everything in the world--the cravings of sinful man, the lust of his eyes and the boasting of what he has and does-- comes not from the Father but from the world. The world and its desires pass away, but the man who does the will of God lives forever."**

90

Does it not seem as if weeds live forever? You just can't seem to kill the suckers. You spray them, pull them up by the roots, and they just keep coming back. Couldn't Jesus use some "weedy" Christians like that? Most of us are too much like pedigree grass that must be pampered with just the right amount of water, fertilizer, and sun. Too much, or too little of any one of those will cause the grass to rebel, wither and go dormant in spite of all its preferential treatment. You've got to hand it to weeds. We spray them with poison, jerk them up by the root, starve them of any nutrients, and yet they not only survive but outgrow and out-shine our pampered purebred grasses.

What's even more amazing is that the church is supposed to be the soil for weeds... those who are despised and rejected by the world. As strange as it may be, we do not seem to want weeds in our church. We want lush green grass. Like grass, most Christians have to be pampered, watered and fed in just the right proportion, or they will wither up and go dormant, too.

What ever happened to commitment and sacrifice for the common good of all? God has called us to be *in* the world but not *of* the world. Jesus said that the world hates Him. If the world hates the Master, how do you think it feels about the servants?

Weeds of Christ, unite! Let us rise up out of the drought of spiritual apathy and flourish as a testimony to the fact that Jesus has made us overcomers! We will prevail! We cannot die but once because we have been born twice. And we *will* live forever! Bless the Lord!

I don't know about you, but I still don't like weeds in my yard. I do, however, cut them down with a lot more respect than I used to. God has used them to encourage me to hang tough... even in dry, wilderness places. The latter rains are on the way, Beloved. Take root and hang on!

37

Where, O death, is your victory? Where, O death, is your sting? The sting of death is sin, and the power of sin is the law. But thanks be to God! He gives us the victory through our Lord Jesus Christ.

---I Corinthians 15:55-56

Pulling weeds can be hazardous. Yesterday while pulling another crop of weeds from our much maligned ditch beside our house, I encountered an angry bumblebee. He flew into my shirt. As I raked him out, he crawled inside my glove. That's when he gave me his best shot... right in he heel of my palm.

What happened next was amazing. I was stung by a bumblebee when I was four years old. I can still remember how badly it hurt. When he stung me this time, I kept waiting for the intense burning pain I remembered from days gone by to begin pulsating through my hand. It never did. I just invoked my covenant privilege... *"Father, I don't receive this pain, because it's not from you."* The pain just never came even though I could see the stinger embedded in my hand.

What happened next brought about a weird

combination of emotions... anger and laughter. I was mad that he had the audacity to sting me when I had done nothing to him. Then I laughed as he kept flying at my head attacking me again. He must have thought I was stupid or something. It doesn't take a rocket scientist to figure out that a bee has only one stinger. After he gives you his best shot, he has nothing more to inflict upon you.

As he kept making his aerial attack, I just grabbed him out of the air and squeezed his guts out. Then I threw him on the ground and stomped him to smitherenes. I felt like a victorious conqueror. Like Rocky dancing on the steps of the capitol building. What a feeling!

In the afterglow of the battle, I realized that the devil is a lot like that bumblebee. One time he stung us with sin bringing pain and death; but Jesus took the pain of that sting for us. The Lord Jesus pulled satan's stinger out once and for all on the cross. Satan is now like that stingerless bumblebee attacking our minds with an aerial display of godless thoughts. His attacks should bring forth anger and laughter within us as well. What we need to do is snatch the prince of the power of the air out of the air and squeeze *his* guts out. Then we should cast him down and stomp him to smitherenes. Put him under our feet just like the song says. If we are seated in the heavenlies in Christ, and everything is under His feet, then satan must be under our feet, too (Ephesians 2:6). Bless the Lord!

There's another thing about the bumblebee. Science affirms that the bumblebee cannot fly. The laws of physics and aerodynamics tell us that a bumblebee's wings are incapable of sustaining his massive body weight in flight. But no one ever told the bumblebee. So, he keeps right on flying.

Satan, like the bumblebee, has no power over us as

children of God. But he doesn't believe that. He keeps right on attacking us even though he is *stingerless*. What's even more amazing is the number of saints, who through the fear of being stung, keep backing down from his attacks. Beloved, he has no power to hurt you anymore. Jesus jerked his stinger out, and all he has to fight with now is fear and intimidation. Grab that sucker out the air and squeeze him to death. Invoke your covenant privilege. ***Submit yourself to God, resist the devil, and he will flee*** (James 4:7).

With no stinger, he's as harmless as a fly. Swat him and let's get on with pulling weeds so the good stuff can grow. Amen? ...Amen!!!

38

He makes me lie down in green pastures.

—Psalm 23:2

Monday was weed day at the Ashley estate. We pulled weeds out of flower beds and gardens until dark. I was reminded of that famous statement, *"The only thing that is needed for evil to triumph is for good men to do nothing."* How true!

We have been so busy lately with Vacation Bible School, counseling, teaching, and such that we have simply neglected our yard work. Due to that negligence, we've had giant weeds growing with taproots that almost reached China. And talk about back-breaking work to get rid of them... Wow! Every time we let those weeds get out of hand, we vow never to let it happen again. But alas, they come springing back up with a vengeance if given even the slightest reprieve.

As we labored, I noticed that the small weeds were easy to pull up, especially after the rains we've had of late. You can just reach down and pluck them right up when they are young, tender and have no deep root. But give them a couple of weeks to grow, and they will break your back tugging on them. Sin, like a weed, is easier to pull up after our soul is soaked in the water of His Spirit. W e need to pull that sin out before our hearts harden like sun-baked clay.

In addition to weeds, there is the menace of Bermuda grass, also known as "devil grass." Have you experienced the pestilence of "devil grass"? This grass grows by leaps and bounds in hot, humid weather. It has long runners with fingers that reach out in all directions. Everywhere it touches the ground it takes root. If left unchecked, it is next to impossible to eradicate short of killing it with Round-Up (a herbicide of the highest order). It is extremely invasive. It will take over flower beds, gardens and anywhere else you don't want it to go. Give it a couple of weeks of growth, and it will overrun you.

Sin is *real* "devil's grass." It crops up in places where you don't want it. Sin is most vulnerable to eradication when you catch it early before the root has a chance to dig deep into the soil of your soul. At the first sign of conviction when your heart is soft and tender is the best time to reach down and pluck it out. But like people who love yard work, Christians become distracted as well. When we don't take time to oversee the garden of our heart, weeds of sin will come in like a flood taking over special ground hitherto reserved for Father God and His purpose for our life. If neglect is protracted, weeds and "devil grass" will overwhelm us to the point of thinking that any effort to get rid of them is futile. We, therefore, become hopeless and think, *"What's the use in trying?"*

Nevertheless, take heart. The devil's greatest fear is the Blood of the Lord Jesus. The Blood of Christ kills sin down to the very hair roots. Satan knows that love grows where the blood falls. Satan thrives on hate. Love nauseates him. That's why he hates the Blood so much. The Blood is spiritual Round-up in the most lethal of concentrations. It annihilates sin, obliterates shame, and decimates guilt. There is tremendous power in the Blood of our Lord Jesus Christ. And Beloved, His Blood flows through your veins. As His child, Jesus is your very life. All that He is, you are. Praise His holy name!

Now understand this. A weed can have some of the prettiest blooms and flowers, but it will still root out the good stuff that should be growing in its place. Don't be deceived by sin's attractiveness. Sin will take over your soul, and root out your destiny. Pull it up before it takes root and chokes out your identity in Christ.

The grass is always greener on Father God's side. Step on in and enjoy the soft, cool feel of His green pastures between your toes. No weeds at all. Go ahead. Wiggle your toes in the lush, thick grass of His grace. Ah.... feels good, doesn't it?

Go ahead and lie down in His green pastures and let Him restore your soul. The rest will do you good!

39

Thou hast enlarged me when I was in distress.
                                                        ---Psalm 4:1 (KJV)

James Michener, the well-known author, was asked one time how he kept writing productively in his advancing years. Michener told about a farmer who did something that inspired him when James was only five years old. It seems that this farmer had an old apple tree whose productivity had declined drastically over the years. One afternoon, the farmer drove eight old rusty nails into the trunk of that apple tree. The next autumn, that old apple tree produced a bumper crop of the most delicious apples you ever tasted.

James asked the farmer how the miracle happened. The farmer explained, *"Hammering the rusty nails gave it a shock to remind it that its job is to produce apples."* (Reader's Digest, Dec. 1993, p.25)

I am writing this story on the day after over two million men gathered to worship God on the mall in Washington, D.C.. In that place, God drove a lot of rusty nails into a lot of unproductive men. It was a shock to us all. There God reminded us that our purpose is to **"bear fruit and that our fruit should remain"** (John 15:16).

Encouragement is a wonderful thing. We all need it. Can't live without it. However, encouragement comes in

97

different packages. Sometimes it comes with a warm embrace. At other times with a word of praise. But oftentimes, encouragement comes in less palatable doses... like rusty nails of reproof and rebuke.

It is easy to hear and not heed... to listen and not live. Too often we become "gospel hardened." We hear the good news so much that we take it for granted. Its freshness becomes stale and brittle.

Allow me to offer a few rusty nails for your encouragement:

- When is the last time you jumped up on your Heavenly Daddy's lap and told Him you loved Him?
- When is the last time you told another person how good God is?
- Did you use words this week that you would never use in front of Jesus?
- Have you been rude or impolite?
- Men, did you honor your wife this week as Christ honors the church? Did you treat her as a prized possession, or as a maid, or a fixture? How often did you tell her you love her in both word and deed? Were you sarcastic at the expense of your Bride?
- Ladies, did you reverence your husband this week? Did you brag on him to others? Did you tell him how wonderful he is? Did you belittle your husband in front of others?
- Children, did you obey your parents this week with a good attitude? Did you express appreciation for all they have done for you?
- Saints, were you faithful to God's church? Did you speak well of the Bride of Christ? Or did you put her down and make judgmental comments about her?

• Did you listen to the Holy Spirit? Did you immediately obey when you heard His voice? Did you give thanks for all things, including the bad things?

I could go on, but the pain maybe getting a little intense. Do you remember the Westminster Shorter Catechism? It states... *"the chief end of man is to glorify God and enjoy Him forever."* Are you doing that?

Beloved, what is your purpose? Your destiny? Why are you here? Why did God create you? He created apple trees to make apples. He created you to bring glory to Him and to simply enjoy Him, not endure Him. Are you doing that?

You say... *"How do I do that?"* It's simple. Let me give you three steps:

1. Obedience.
2. Obedience.
3. Obedience.

Did you get those? We glorify God by being obedient. Jesus said, ***"If you love Me, keep My commandments"*** (John 14:15).

We live in a world system that perpetuates selfishness, ego, pride, and independence. It's all too easy to get dirty and polluted from merely walking in the world every day. Thank God for those rusty nails that remind us of our destiny as His children. Let us not gripe and complain when God encourages us with painful trials. Instead, let us give thanks and praise for those gracious reminders.

Right now, I am reminded of three rusty nails that pinned our Lord and Savior to a tree 2000 years ago. Those nails were a shock to His body, too. But, wow! Look at the fruit they produced... and are still producing!

Because He took those rusty nails for me, I am the apple of His eye! And so are you!

40

And Jesus said to them, "Take off the graveclothes and let him go."

—John 11:44

What does an acorn and a one hundred year old oak tree have in common? They are both pure, unadulterated oaks through and through. Every cell in both the acorn and the full grown tree is the same. Oak. Whole oak. Nothing but oak. There is no pear tree, monkey grass, or grapevine in their composition. Just oak. Pure and simple.

Have you ever made the statement: *"I want to be more like Jesus?"* Well, if you are a blood-bought, born-again child of God, that is an impossibility. You cannot be more like Jesus than you already are. Every shred of your spirit is Jesus' Life. The Greek word for His Life imparted to you is *"zoe."* Jesus said that He came to give us Life (zoe) and Life (zoe) more abundantly. You are a new creation. Old things haves passed away. All things in your spirit have become new.

God's Word tells us that we are made complete in Christ (Colossians 2:10). We have been given every spiritual blessing in Christ (Ephesians 1:3). He has given to us everything we need for Life (zoe) and godliness (2 Peter

1:3). In Him was Life (zoe) and that Life (zoe) was the light of men (John 1:4). Jesus said that we were the light of the world (Matthew 5:14). If His Life is light and that light is in us, how can we shine if we are not the essence of His Life (zoe)?

Beloved, we are seeking the wrong thing. We do not need to be more like Christ. We are like Christ in every way in our spirits. We are new creations... just like Jesus. However, we have hardened hearts and unsurrendered souls that keep His Life from shining forth. What we really desire is to be more free.

Sin, selfishness, and fear block and hinder His Life from manifesting through us. These are the graveclothes of the *"old man"* we were before Christ gave us Life (zoe).

Let me ask you something. How alive was Lazarus when Jesus called him out of the tomb? As alive as he could be. However, his resurrected Life was still bound by graveclothes. He could not live and move freely in that new Life. All of us to a certain extent are bound with the shroud of fear, unbelief, confusion, and sin. What we need is to be more free... free from the things that bind us so that His Life can consume us and manifest through us.

God created us to soar like eagles, but most of us live like turkeys... heads down, pecking the ground. Beloved, you were made to fly. Spread those wings of trust and obey today and head right into the winds of fear and doubt. Be free today! Walk in the freedom that Jesus died to give you. ***"If the Son shall make you free, you shall be free indeed"*** (John 8:36).

You may only be a little acorn today with a lot of growing to do. Nevertheless, you are a mighty oak of righteousness through and through. Before you can spring up mightily, you must become like the acorn. Every mighty oak was once an acorn that fell into the ground and died. But from that death came life. Life many times greater than the acorn could have ever imagined.

Think about that the next time you reach out your branches and give shade to a fellow wilderness wanderer who is tired and weary. That is your destiny, Beloved. Ours is the same as His. Be rooted and grounded in Him today.

41

I praise You because I am fearfully and wonderfully made; Your works are wonderful, I know that full well.

---Psalm 139:14

Our God is an awesome God! We sometimes think that He is too big and awesome to care about us, but the Bible clearly states otherwise. Heavenly Father is concerned about every minute detail of our lives. David said, *"How precious to me are Your thoughts, O God! How vast the sum of them! Were I to count them, they would outnumber the grains of sand"* (Psalm 139:17). Now does that sound like a God who does not care for you? I don't think so.

He is so concerned about you that He numbers every hair on your head individually (Matthew 10:30). No, He does not merely know how many hairs are on your head. He has each one numbered. He knows that numbers 139, 268, 498, and 598 went down the drain this morning when you took your shower. How's that for being interested?

Father constantly watches over us... protects us... anticipates our every need. Sometimes when I think God has forgotten me, He reminds me that I'm not a better Daddy than He is. I get a bit audacious sometimes and think that I love and care for my children more than He loves me. Then he gently rebukes me... chastens me... and loves me.

He reminded me the other day that He knows I would lose my head if it wasn't tied on. He takes care of some of my most essential needs automatically. Thank the Lord, He does! Let me show you...

Every day Father God takes care of a normal middle-aged man in the following ways: His heart beats 103,680 times... His blood circulates throughout his body every 23 seconds and travels 43 million miles a day... He breathes 23,000 times... He inhales 438 cubic feet of air... He digests 3.25 pounds of food... He assimilates over one half gallon of liquid... He evaporates 2 pounds of water through perspiration... He generates 98.6 degrees of heat... He uses 450 tons of energy... His hair grows 1/100 of an inch... His fingernails grow 1/200 of an inch... And he uses 7 million brain cells... ALL AUTOMATICALLY!!!

Beloved, if Father God loves you enough to keep you up and running every minute of every day, do you not think He will take care of the other things that you are worrying about? He knows your every need. He has a solution before you ever know that you have a problem.

Relax... Father knows best! Get to the place where you trust Him... ***automatically!***

42

But thanks be to God, Who always causes us to triumph in Christ...

---2 Corinthians 2:14

I heard a story once about a man who raised and trained champion hunting dogs. His dogs were famous, and his reputation was world renown. One day his son found a stray puppy. He brought him home and showed the dog to his father. The father said, *"Son, that dog is nothing but an old biscuit-eater. He'll never amount to anything."*

Every time that stray would come around the boy's father, the man would stomp his foot and yell at the dog, *"Get out of here, you old biscuit-eater!"* The dog would cower down, tuck his tail between his legs and trot away.

Nevertheless, the boy loved that old dog. Having watched his dad train champions for years, the boy had become a pretty proficient dog trainer in his own right. So, he began to train his little biscuit-eater on his own.

One day, the national championships were being held and to the surprise of the father, the boy entered his stray in the contest. The dad was furious. *"Son, why do you want to embarrass the family like that. That old biscuit-eater can't hunt. He's just an old worthless stray."* But the boy stood firm, and the dad consented. *"If you want to make a fool of yourself, go ahead,"* the father said.

As the competition progressed, the old stray outperformed them all. Going into the final round of competition, the boy's dog was light years ahead of the field. Dad came to talk with his son. *"Son, what are you doing. If I lose this competition, our livelihood and my reputation is gone. That old stray is not a champion. He's a loser... a plain old biscuit-eater. He will never be a champion."* The dad stomped his foot and yelled at the stray, *"Get out of here you old biscuit-eater!"* The poor little dog cowered down, tucked his tail and trotted away.

The father kept his reputation that day, but lost his son. It's amazing the price some are willing to pay for things we cannot keep while throwing away our priceless treasures.

There are many biscuit-eaters in this world. People who are precious to the Master, but who have been programmed to believe that they are no good biscuit-eaters. Many walk around today all cowered down, tail between their legs, and plodding through life with no joy, love, and peace--- all because they have believed the lie of the devil. Old slewfoot stomps his foot, and they tuck tail and run.

But take heart. Way back in Genesis, Father told us that satan might stomp at us, but one day Jesus would stomp his head and crush him. At the cross, Jesus broke the authority of satan. And on that Sunday morning when Lord Jesus came bursting out of the tomb, He crushed satan's ugly head once and for all with one big stomp of His foot. Praise the Lord! It's time that we stomp our foot at the devil and send him to the pit with his tail between his legs.

Beloved, because Jesus is alive, all is forgiven. You're not a biscuit-eater. You're a champion. A King's Kid. You're not a sinner. You're a saint who occasionally sins. You're a priceless, blood-bought child of Father God... dearly loved. You have been washed in the blood of the Lamb. You wear the robe of His righteousness. You wear the ring of His authority. To Father, you're the best He ever saw. You are the apple of His eye. You are absolutely, totally forgiven and accepted. Rejoice! You're a child of the consummate Champion over sin, death, and the devil. Rise up, O biscuit-eaters! A feast awaits. Come and enjoy. Hold your head up high. Your redemption draweth nigh! Rejoice and be glad. He is risen! We are forgiven! Hallelujah to the King Victorious!

Because He is living and reigning today, everything is under His feet. Because we are IN Him, everything is under our feet as well. It's time you put your foot down!

43

Jesus replied: "Love the Lord your God with all your heart and with all your soul and with all your mind." This is the first and greatest commandment.

---Matthew 22:37-38

How's your love life? Yeah, your love life. How is it? The Lord asked me to examine mine this morning. He asked me to compare my love relationship with my Bride with my love for Him. I thought it a strange request until I began to make a closer examination.

Understand now, I have the sweetest, most wonderful, most precious Bride that God ever created. No, I'm not prejudiced. I know what I know. And if you guys don't feel the same way about your Bride, then something is wrong with you.

Something was wrong with me a few years ago. I did not always love her that way. Oh, I loved her with all my heart, but I was so clogged up with hurts, wounds, selfishness, sin, unbelief and disobedience that I could not get that love to her in any significant amount.

Then one day, God miraculously healed me and my Bride. He just came and washed us, cleansed us, shined us up, changed our oil, tuned us up, and set us loose. We fell "head-over-heels" in love all over again. It was wonderful. It cannot be explained except that God just showered us with His love and grace. He opened a wellspring of His Life in us and His river of love just keeps flowing.

Now, I cannot stand to be apart from her. When I see her, it's like seeing her for the first time. I'm amazed that out of all this world (and she could have had the best), she chose me. It boggles my mind. I just want to be with her. If I'm sitting on the couch, I want her right beside me. If I go to Wal Mart, I want her to ride with me. I can't keep my hands off of her. I hold her hand when we ride in the car. I have to touch her hair, hug her neck, or kiss her every time I'm around her. I love my Bride.

Then, I heard Him say, **"Kenny, do you love Me?"**

"Yes, Lord, you know that I love You. Don't You?" I replied dubiously.

Then He got quiet. I hate it when He gets quiet. I began to examine my love for Him compared to my love for

Wanda. I do love the Lord, but I had to admit that my love for Him was more of a service *to* than a love *for* Him. When I come into His presence, I don't look at Him as if seeing Him for the first time. When I come into His presence, I have an agenda. I have requests. I have needs to be met. I have questions I need answered. When I know I'm going to see Him, I don't feel butterflies in my stomach like I do with Wanda.

I began wondering what kind of relationship Wanda and I would have if I loved her like I was loving the Lord and vice versa. Imagine a typical conversation (prayer if you will) if Wanda was the Lord.

"Thank you so much for loving me and putting up with me. Honey, how can I serve you today? What can I do for you? Wash dishes? Vacuum the house? Weed the garden? Convert our entire county? Set all the emotionally oppressed free? Whatever you need me to do, I'm here. Okay? Now, I need you to do some things for me. Would you bless my elders and deacons today? Put the words in my mouth when I counsel? Give me a message for the people this week? Thank you so much for loving me and listening to me. I'll get these things done for you right away. I'll see you tomorrow."

What if Wanda treated me that way? It would break my heart. I don't want her to leave me to do things for me. I want her. I want to touch her... Hold her... Love her... Talk with her... Be with her... I don't want her doing stuff *for* me if it's going to take her away *from* me.

Then all of a sudden, I heard this Holy voice, **"Bingo! You've got it. Now, you understand how I feel?"**

Right then and there, I remembered that the greatest commandment was not to *serve* the Lord with all my heart. It was to *love* Him with all my heart. Jesus said that if we loved Him, we should keep His commandments. I had kept a lot of His commandments and lost sight of the greatest one of all... simply to love Him.

I understood, but I could not help wondering where the service came in. If I spent all my time with the Lord, how could I help others come to know and love Him? No sooner had the thought entered my mind when I heard one of my elders pray: *"Lord, thank you for what you have done in my pastor and his wife. It blesses my heart when I see him hug her, hold her hand and love her. It encourages me to love my wife that way, too."*

That was my answer. Our service comes as a result of our love for Him. I didn't do anything but love my Bride, and that encouraged another to do likewise. I guess it's like the old adage: I hear... *I forget.* I see... *I remember.* I do... *I understand.*

What is the objective of ministry anyway? To get people to fall "head-over-heels" in love with Jesus. Right? Well, the best way to do that is to model it, not talk about it. Some of the most precious times I've ever had with my Bride are times when we don't talk at all. We just enjoy being with each other.

Father gently reminded me this morning how much he misses me. He misses you, too. Why don't you drop your agenda today and go for a ride with the Lord. And let Him hold **your** hand on the way.

44

The LORD your God is with you, He is mighty to save. He will take great delight in you, He will quiet you with His love, He will rejoice over you with singing.

---Zephaniah 3:17

As I have mentioned on several occasions, Dennis Jernigan is the most anointed Christian song writer in the universe. God miraculously delivered him from the wilderness and gave him a beautiful Bride and at last count, nine wonderful children. He knows how amazing grace really is. He is desperately in love with Jesus. His songs are evidence of His great love for Father God.

His favorite verse of Scripture is Zephaniah 3:17. Dennis has expounded his own translation of that verse based on his knowledge of the Father heart of God. It goes like this:

"The eternal self-existent God... the God Who is three in one. He Who dwells in the center of your being is a powerful valiant warrior. He has come to set you free... to keep you safe and to bring you victory. He is cheered, and He beams with exceeding joy and takes pleasure in your presence. He has engraved a place for Himself in you, and there He quietly rests in His love and affection for you. He

cannot contain Himself at the thought of you and with the greatest of joy spins around wildly in anticipation over you and has placed you above all other creations and in the highest place of His priorities. In fact, He shouts and sings in triumph, joyfully proclaiming the gladness of His heart in a song of rejoicing. All because of you. " (Heartcry Music, words and music by Dennis Jernigan)

Beloved, that is what God thinks of you and me. He loves us absolutely perfectly. He delights to be in your presence. Can you imagine that? It blesses His heart when you stop and take time to share your day with Him.

You don't understand how He could love you so much? Well, let me ask you this. Do you understand how that cheeseburger, or whatever you love to eat, passes into your stomach, is converted into energy and nutrients and gets to every cell of your body so that you can live and move and have your being? Even if you are a microbiologist, you probably still do not understand that mystery in its entirety. I don't understand it myself, but my lack of understanding has never stopped me from eating cheeseburgers.

Eating... That reminds me of a story.

Once upon a time, a lady came down with a terminal disease. She approached her pastor in order to make arrangements for her funeral. She requested that when she was placed in her casket, her Bible be placed in one hand and a fork in the other.

The pastor was quite puzzled and inquired of the lady the reason for the fork. She said, *"Pastor, the Word of God has always been the main course for me. It has given me balanced nutrition for my spiritual walk with Christ all of these years. It has been like honey from the rock. Spiritually, I am stronger and more vibrant than I have ever been. But Pastor, you know how we love to eat at church. At every church dinner, when they come by to take your plate, they always whisper, 'Keep your fork. You don't want to miss dessert.' And you know how good the desserts are in our church. Umm... Umm! Well, you see, I believe the best is yet to come for me. Jesus has been so good to me here on earth, but I believe He is saving the best for last. I am going to see Him face to face. That's one dessert I'm not going to miss. So, when people ask about my fork, just tell them that the best is yet to come."* (author unknown).

Beloved, keep **your** fork today!

45

What things soever ye desire, when you pray, believe that you receive them, and you will have them.

---Mark 11:24(KJV)

Iwas talking to my Heavenly Father the other day about some concerns I've had. I was wondering why so few prayers were being answered when so many prayers were being prayed. He then began to show me the reason. He will always tell you what you want if you really want to know.

God began to teach me about real faith... the kind that moves mountains and glorifies God. The first verse He showed me was Mark 11:24. I said, *"Lord, do you mean that if I believe that I have, right now, what I am asking for, then*

I will have it?"

He replied, **"Isn't that what I said?"**

Then He showed me Hebrews 11:1... ***"Now faith is the SUBSTANCE of things hoped for, and the evidence of things not seen."*** I said, *"Lord, do You mean if I have faith, then I have the substance, even if I cannot see it, feel it, touch it, taste it, or smell it?"*

He said, **"You got it!"**

Romans 4:17 says, ***"...God, Who gives life to the dead and calls those things which do not exist as though they did."*** God sees me as I **shall be**, not just as I am. God practices what He preaches. We should do likewise.

When Abraham was 75 years old, God told Abraham that he would have a son even though Sarah was barren. He had the promise of God. He also had circumstances in his life that were diametrically opposed to that promise. For 25 years, he waited and wondered about God's promise. Then one day, this is what he did. ***"For Abraham, human reason for hope being gone, hoped in faith that he should become the father of many nations, as he had been promised, 'So numberless shall your descendants be'"*** (Romans 4:18).

Abraham followed God's example. He called those things that be not as though they were. He proclaimed, *"I am a Daddy!"* Nine months later, he was!

Could it be the reason we do not receive answers to our prayers is that we do not exercise biblical faith? Do we believe that we have the things we pray for before we actually get them? That's God's way. If we pray God's way, then prayer is effectual and glorifying to God.

Isn't it time we started taking God seriously? To live in the fulness of God is God's will for all His children. That is the normal Christian life. However, we have been *subnormal* for so long that if we ever became *normal* the world would think we were *abnormal*. We have an abnormally awesome God. He expects His children who are made in His image to be just like him. Dare to be a normal Christian. Take God at His Word. Faith is the key that unlocks the promises of God in the normal Christian life.

In John Bunyan's classic, **_Pilgrim's Progress_**, Christian took the wrong road and was captured by Giant Despair. The Giant locked Christian and Hopeful, his companion, in the dungeon of Doubting Castle. Everyday, Giant Despair would come and beat them both. Christian and Hopeful, weak from lack of food and the beatings, despaired even of life. Giant Despair counseled them to commit suicide to alleviate their suffering.

Christian was ready to heed the Giant's counsel, but Hopeful kept encouraging him not to give up. Then when things looked their worst, Christian and Hopeful prayed all night. About daybreak, the Holy Spirit reminded Christian about the key in his vest pocket... a key called "Promise."

Hopeful said, *"Well, Christian, what are you waiting for?" Unlock that door and let's get out of here."* Christian slipped the key into the lock and with a twist of faith, unlocked the door. They were free.

How sad that Christian had the key of Promise in his pocket all the time but failed to use it. How sad that we, children of the King, have His promises as well and either due to ignorance, or lack of faith, never stand upon them.

Beloved, all the promises of God are for you. They are inscribed upon your heart. Why not whip them out right now and with a twist of faith call them into being. You can do it. God has given to each of us a measure of faith along with the key of Promise. Haven't you spent enough time bleeding and starving in the dungeon of Doubting Castle?

114

Pull that promise out of your heart, give it a twist of faith, and watch that door swing open. ***"Abraham did not stagger at the promise of God through unbelief, but was strong in faith, giving glory to God, and being fully persuaded that what He had promised, He was also able to perform"*** (Romans 4:20-21).

Abraham is the father of our faith. We are sons and daughters of Abraham. Be a chip off the old block and quit staggering in unbelief. Step out on God's promises today. You won't sink. I guarantee it! He's never let me down! He'll be there for you, too!

Now, where did I leave those keys?

46

And let us not lose heart and grow weary and faint in acting nobly and doing right, for in due time and at the appointed season we shall reap, if we do not loosen and relax our courage and faint.

---Galatians 6:9

The other night in our men's meeting while we were praying, the Lord showed me something about perseverance in prayer. I have often wondered why some of our prayers are answered immediately while others take days, months, or even years to be answered. He reminded me of Rocky Balboa. Rocky did not knock out Apollo Creed with one punch. Apollo was a powerful adversary. Rocky took a licking but kept on ticking. He kept punching when every fiber of his being told him to quit. But he kept hanging on ... round after round.

In the final round, Rocky hit Apollo and hurt him. His knees buckled. Suddenly, adrenalin and hope flooded Rocky's soul. He began to punch with renewed power and energy. Finally, with all his might he landed one last blow with such force that both he and Apollo hit the canvas simultaneously. Both tried desperately to get up. Apollo didn't make it. Rocky stood at the count of 9. Rocky persevered and won!

I guess you wonder what's the point of this story. **Revelation 5:8** says, *"He came and took the scroll from the right hand of Him who sat on the throne. And when he had taken it, the four living creatures and the twenty-four elders fell down before the Lamb. Each one had a harp and they were holding golden bowls full of incense, which are the prayers of the saints."* Revelation **8:3-5** goes on to say, *"Another angel, who had a golden censer, came and stood at the altar. He was given much incense to offer, with the prayers of all the saints, on the golden altar before the throne. The smoke of the incense, together with the prayers of the saints, went up before God from the angel's hand. Then the angel took the censer, filled it with fire from the altar, and hurled it on the earth; and there came peals of thunder, rumblings, flashes of lightning and an earthquake."*

In heaven, there are bowls which collect our prayers. When those bowls are full, God mixes them with fire and hurls them to earth. These are prayers answered and filled with the power of Almighty God. Whenever the time is right, and there are enough prayers to fill the bowls, God releases His power and accomplishes His purposes.

God takes the same fire that burned on Mt. Sinai... the same fire that consumed Elijah's water and rocks on Mt. Carmel... the same fire that fell at Pentecost... the same fire that destroyed His enemies... the very fire of our God Who is a consuming fire, and mixes it with our prayers and pours it out on the earth. Lightning. Thunder. Earthquakes. The earth shakes at the sound of His voice. The nations tremble before Him. The idols of man crash at the feet of the Lord our God.

Do you see now why we must keep on praying no matter what? There are various levels of power needed for different situations. For example, can you light a flashlight with 2 flashlight batteries? Yes. Can you light a city with 2 flashlight batteries? No. Different situations require different power levels. That's why the disciples could cast out some demons but were unable to cast out the demon in the boy after Jesus came down from the Mount of Transfiguration.

Let me encourage you as God has encouraged me. Don't think that your prayers are in vain, or that God is reluctant to answer. Picture your prayers like a pump air rifle. The more you pump the lever, the more pressure builds and the more powerfully the BB is hurled. Every prayer is like a pump on the air rifle. Every prayer builds up power and pressure. When God knows that the power is sufficient to overcome the adversary, He mixes those pumped up prayers with His holy fire and hurls that bullet to earth, striking the enemy in the heart and setting the captives free, opening the eyes of the blind and healing the sick.

That's what happened when Paul and Silas were in jail singing and praising God. Worship ascended... God anointed it... the bowls filled... God poured it out... the earth shook... their shackles fell off... the jailer was saved... and many were born again in Philippi.

Don't give up, Beloved. Every prayer adds power and fills your bowl a little bit more. The more you pray the faster your bowl fills. Pray without ceasing. And don't faint. Like Rocky, all God asks from us is to be standing when the bell rings at the end of the last round. He'll do the rest. And remember... we stand tallest when on our knees.

Keep your guard up... and keep punching! I just saw the devil's knees buckle!

47

Don't be afraid; from now on you will catch men.

---Luke 5:10

Remember the story about Fred, the fisherman? Fred was catching a mess of fish when nobody else was even getting a bite. Fred would come in everyday with his boat full of fish. People were really upset that Fred kept his fishing holes and secrets so guarded.

Then one day, the game warden came to see Fred and inquired about the secret of his success. Fred invited the warden to accompany him for a day of fishing. Once they were out on the lake and anchored down, Fred pulled out a stick of dynamite. As Fred was lighting the dynamite, the warden cried out, *"Fred, what are you doing!"*

"I'm fishing!" Fred calmly replied.

"You can't do that! That's illegal, not to mention dangerous!" screamed the hysterical warden.

About that time, Fred tossed the lighted stick of dynamite into the warden's lap and said, *"You gonna fuss, or you gonna fish?"*

That funny little story tickles us, but it has implications as to what God is up to in His world these days. The Word of God tells us in Luke 10:19 (KJV), **"Behold, I give unto you** power **to tread on serpents and scorpions, and over all the** power **of the enemy: and nothing shall by any means hurt you."** The Greek word for **power** is **dunamis** from which we derive our word, *dynamite*. Jesus has given us dynamite power to tread upon the enemy of our souls. The word means *"inherent power, power residing in a thing by virtue of its nature."*

Paul was trying to wake up the Ephesians like Fred was trying to wake up the game warden. Paul knew the nature of the power each and every believer possesses due to the fact that Jesus is our very Life. His nature is our nature. Paul says, **"I pray also that the eyes of your heart may be enlightened in order that you may know the hope to which He has called you, the riches of His glorious inheritance in the saints, and His incomparably great power (dunamis) for us who believe. That** power **is like the working of His mighty strength, which He exerted in Christ when He raised Him from the dead and seated Him at His right hand in the heavenly realms, far above all rule and authority, power and dominion, and every title that can be given, not only in the present age but**

also in the one to come" (Ephesians 1:18-21).

Do you see that, Beloved? The same power that raised Jesus from the dead is in you and me! That power is inherent in you. It is your very nature. Why are we not unleashing that power upon a lost and dying world to set them free by the grace and mercy of the Lord?

I believe that one reason we are not living powerful lives is because we have been told that it is illegal. Religion has kept us captive for so long. We have been told that anything outside of the boundary of our religion is of the devil... illegal so to speak. Some of us have been taught that it is illegal to do any of these things: raise your hands in praise... clap in church... dance in the Spirit... pray for people in restaurants... publicly rebuke ungodly behavior... smile all the time... hug people with AIDS... love sinners and hate sin... ad infinitum.

The Apostle Paul said, ***"All things are lawful unto me, but all things are not expedient: all things are lawful for me, but I will not be brought under the power of any"*** (I Corinthians 6:12 KJV). Beloved, Jesus set us free from the laws with which people and institutions imprison us. If the Son sets you free, then you are free indeed. Not only did He set us free, He empowered us... commissioned us... ordained us... to go and set the captives free, to heal the broken-hearted, to bind up the wounded, to proclaim liberty to the captives.

You want so much for Jesus to be real to you, don't you? Want to know how? Simply unleash His power that is inherent in you. There are three steps. Ready? OBEDIENCE... OBEDIENCE... OBEDIENCE! Did you get that? The next time the Holy Spirit prompts you to go speak to someone, do it. When the Spirit whispers, *"Give Sue a call,"* drop whatever you are doing and call Sue. When you feel His love rising within you during worship, lift your hands and give Him all your praise and worship. Quit worrying about what people think. You flatter yourself by believing that people think that much about you. They don't.

Beloved, focus on Jesus. Be obedient. Love Him. Praise Him. If you do, your boat will soon be filling up with blessings like Fred's.

God has called and empowered us to be *"fishers of men."* Now, what are you gonna do? You gonna fuss, or you gonna fish?

48

Before every man there lies a wide and pleasant road that seems right but ends in death.

---Proverbs 14:12 (Living Bible)

Once upon a time, there were two bosom buddies---an eagle and a chicken. They were almost inseparable. They flew everywhere together. One day while flying the friendly skies, the chicken said to the eagle, *"I'm starving. Why don't we land and get a bite to eat."*

"Sounds good to me," said the eagle and down they swooped. It just so happened that they landed near a cow eating corn out in the field. They were amazed that the cow

offered to share her corn with them. Usually they had to hunt and fight for their food.

The eagle cautiously asked, *"How come you're so willing to share your food with us?"*

"Oh, we have plenty to eat here. The farmer brings it to us everyday... all we want. We live over there in the big barn that shelters us from the weather. We don't have to lift a finger here," said the cow.

"WOW!" exclaimed the chicken. *"We've always had to search for our food and shelter."*

The chicken pulled the eagle aside and said, *"Why don't we stay here. Plenty of food and shelter. No more having to work for a living. How about it?"*

The eagle said, *"I don't know about all this. It sounds too good to be true. Besides, I kinda like flying high and free. And I enjoy the challenge of hunting for my own food and shelter."*

Well, the chicken decided to stay while the eagle decided he loved his freedom too much to give it up for a free meal. So, the eagle took off and the chicken stayed behind.

Everything went great for the chicken... for a while. He ate all he wanted. He grew fat and lazy. Then one day, he overheard the farmer tell his wife to kill the chicken for dinner because the preacher was coming over. The chicken decided it was time to rejoin his friend, the eagle. However, by this time he had grown too fat and weak to fly. Now, he could only flutter. The next day, the farmer and the preacher sat down to fried chicken.

Proverbs 14:12 in the Living Bible says, ***"Before every man there lies a wide and pleasant road that seems right but ends in death."*** We cannot give up our freedom and liberty for a false sense of security. Compromise today and tomorrow you'll be too fat and weak to **"mount up with wings as eagles."**

You must keep both wings (trust and obey) spread out wide in order to fly. If you don't, you'll end up trying to flutter away from the enemy of your soul who wants to have **YOU** for lunch!

49

For in the same way that you judge others, you will be judged...

—Matthew 7:2

On September 13, 1992 an interesting article appeared in the Houston Chronicle. It seems that a man was given a parking ticket in Los Angeles for being illegally parked. The man was sitting behind the wheel of the car when the officer gave him a ticket. The man did not object, because he was, indeed, illegally parked. The officer simply slipped the thirty dollar ticket on the dash of the car and went on his way.

It's a small wonder that the man just didn't move the car, or at least speak to the officer. He couldn't have done either. He had been dead for 10 to 12 hours.

As strange as it may be, the officer shares a common trait with many Christians. We constantly walk around looking for people who are doing something illegal... hair too long, dress too short, skin the wrong color, home on the wrong side of town. We then put a citation (gossip or criticism) on their dashboard and go off looking for others that we can "straighten out."

How can we walk through life citing others with petty violations and never notice that they are spiritually dead? How can we expect non-Christians to act more "Christ-like" when they do not have the power of His Spirit with which to change? They know they are illegally parked and most won't put up an argument about it. Maybe they would come alive and move their vehicles if we were more concerned about their souls than we are about their behavior.

Christ paid my citation. My guess is that He paid for yours, too. There's probably some guy out there today who would love to know where he can get his citation paid as well. Today, why not check the driver before you pull out your ticket book. He may just need a "jump-start" in Jesus' Name.

50

And we, who with unveiled faces all reflect the Lord's glory, are being transformed into His likeness with ever-increasing glory, which comes from the Lord, Who is the Spirit.

---2 Corinthians 3:18

This morning as I left for the office, the Lord greeted me with a love note... a beautiful orange butterfly. It was as if the Lord was saying, **"Good morning, Kenny! Just want you to know that I love you today and that I will be with you all day long. Have a great day!"**

Have you ever pondered why He made butterflies? They really serve no useful purpose other than blessing us with their beauty. Ever wonder if God just made them in order to remind us of His glory and His great love for us? I do. All the time.

When I saw the butterfly, His Spirit immediately brought our verse for today to mind. We are all in transformation... just like that butterfly. The butterfly had a long, tedious and dangerous journey to reach his beautiful state. He started out as a caterpillar. Ugly. Fuzzy. Girls hated him. Guys stomped on him. Not much fun being a caterpillar. Then one day, he couldn't take the abuse anymore. He wrapped himself in a cocoon. Dark. Lonely. Hidden from sight.

It was in the darkness of that tomb that a grand transformation took place. By a mind-boggling miracle of God, a tremendous metamorphosis transpired. A totally different creature was born. The cocoon began to crack. The new creature clawed, scratched, and stretched for the light. After a time of struggling to free himself from a prison of his on doing, he emerged. Bold. Beautiful. Free. Lighter than air. Transformed. It was worth the wilderness journey.

We have a lot in common with the butterfly, don't we? At one time, we were just like him. Ugly. Fuzzy. Girls hated us. Guys stomped us. It wasn't much fun being a fallen human in a cruel world. Even though we may have given our hearts to Christ and belonged to Him, we still lived a caterpillar existence far short of God's ultimate intention.

Most of us who are butterflies today have at one time or another experienced the "dark night of the soul"... the human equivalent of the caterpillar's cocoon. We became so afraid... so hurt... so angry... so alone. We wrapped ourselves in a shell of self-pity. But the darkness of our tomb could not stem the tide of grief and despair in our souls.

Then somehow, Jesus came. Somehow, He knew what we were feeling. Somehow, He got our attention. His Light dispelled every shadow of darkness. The same power that raised Him from the dead entered our tomb and transformed death into life... His Life. Beautiful! Magnificent! Breath-taking!

The tomb could not hold us. Just as the stone was rolled away from His tomb, He came an opened ours. At first, it was difficult. There was only a little crack. But as we clawed, scratched, and stretched, we finally broke free from the tomb of self, doubt and despair. Now, we are free! The view is so much better from up here. The nectar of Life is so sweet and abundant. God is so good!

Some of you reading this are far removed from that blissful state. Some of you are still crawling around on the ground dodging feet and eating dust. Some of you are tucked away in your own tomb of despair.

Beloved, take heart. Those are vital stages on your wilderness journey to freedom and light. Even when God comes and cracks your tomb, you still need the struggle to make you strong. Don't pray to be released. Wait on God's timing. I know that's tough. Been there... done that. But the struggle makes you strong. The struggle makes you distrust your own strength and trust in His. God has you right where He wants you. He will not leave you, nor forsake you. He loves you.

126

While the darkness enfolds you, reflect on Him... His glory... His love. As you do, you will be transformed into His likeness with ever-increasing glory. Here's the best news of all. The butterfly stage is just the beginning. It gets better everyday. Spread your wings and enjoy your freedom. Jesus just may send you to be a love note to one of His caterpillars today!

51

Let us not give up meeting together, as some are in the habit of doing, but let us encourage one another— and all the more as you see the Day approaching.
—Hebrews 10:25

Snuggles usually doesn't get me up before 6:45 am. However, she's had a roommate this past week named Isaac. They arise early to get in a full day of "horsing around" (or is that "dogging it?"). Anyway, they got me up early, and I got a little perturbed. What I didn't know was that the Lord wanted to show me one of my most favorite things... a gaggle of geese. Yes, a gaggle; not a flock.

While standing out in the yard with my dogs, I heard the clamor of honks coming over the woods behind the house. Suddenly, there they were... flying overhead in a perfect "V" formation. It was spectacular.

Did you know that God programmed them to fly in "V" formation? That's right. In "V" formation, the goose in front creates an uplift for the goose right behind him. By flying in "V" formation, the gaggle can fly at least 71% farther than they could flying alone. Neat, isn't it?

God wants His children to fly in formation as well. Our gaggle is called the "ecclesia," or the "called out ones," or more commonly, the Church. We share a common direction and sense of community. We can get where we are going quicker and easier if we travel on each other's thrust.

Whenever a goose falls out of formation, it suddenly feels the drag and resistance of trying to go it alone. Hence, he quickly gets back into formation to take advantage of the lifting power of the goose in front of him. We need to stay in formation with people who are going in the same direction as we are. You can become worn out very quickly trying to make it on your own. We need each other.

When the lead goose gets tired, he rotates to the back and another goose flies to the point. We need to remember that it pays to take turns doing the hard jobs. Let's quit letting the "faithful few" carry the brunt of service while we savor the benefits of their sacrifice. Let's all take our turn in His service. Realizing the benefit of teamwork, the geese in the back constantly honk to encourage those up front to keep on keeping on. We need to remember that all of us need encouragement and assistance if we are to make it to the Promised Land.

Geese are also inspiring models of loyalty and devotion. When one goose gets sick, or is wounded by a gun shot and falls out of formation, two geese will fall out with him and follow him down to help and protect him. They stay with him until he is able to fly, or until he is dead.

Then they launch out on their own and join another formation to catch up with their group. Father God has a lot of wounded people in His gaggle. Should we not be just as faithful to care for those who have been wounded by the hunter and destroyer of our souls?

Honk! Honk! Keep on flapping up there. You make my flight a lot more enjoyable! And remember, the joy is in the journey... not just the destination! Have a nice flight!

52

Be still, and know that I am God.

---Psalm 46:10a

Have you ever closed your eyes while facing the light and saw little squiggly, hair-like "thing-a-ma-bobs" floating through your eyes? I have. They scared me for a long time. I thought I was weird. Then I got up enough nerve to ask my eye doctor if I was going blind. He assured me that a lot of people have "floaters."

"Floaters" are little flecks of deteriorated eye tissue that break off inside the eye due to aging. They float around inside the vitreous humor of the eye. They can be very distracting. When you close your eyes and try to sleep or pray, "floaters" will grab your attention and keep your mind off the business at hand.

The only way to get rid of floaters is to be still long enough for them to settle. When you look around, they get all stirred up. Our spiritual vision can become distorted when the "floaters" of carnal pursuits begin to flake off and cloud the eyes of our faith.

The cure? Be still. The reason why most of us are almost blind spiritually is because we cannot be still long enough for the "floaters" to settle out. Time spent allowing the "floaters" to settle is not wasted time. It is essential. You wouldn't think about waxing your car before washing it, would you? Well, we have to be cleansed, too, from all fleshly distractions before His glory can shine through.

How's your prayer life? If it's like mine, you run before God, dump your wish list on Him, and run out to get busy with your own agenda. I do all the talking, and God never gets a Word in edge-wise. How many friends would you have if you treated them like that? God gave us two ears and one mouth. That should tell us something about how much we should listen, and how much we should talk.

I am reminded of S.D. Gordon's reflections in his book, <u>Quiet Talks On Prayer</u>. Gordon says that in prayer, the ear is the most important organ because the ear leads the way to the tongue. The mind is largely molded through the ear and the eye. What the ear lets in, the mind works over, and the tongue gives out. Since the power of life and death resides in the tongue, it is crucial to guard what enters our eyes and ears.

It is interesting to note that the men who have known God the best have been the mightiest in prayer. They seemed to be extremely sensitive to Him. What was their secret? They were great listeners to God's voice.

The story is told of a famous artist who invited a friend to his home to view a painting that he had just finished. As the friend entered the artist's home, an attendant led him to a room which was quite dark and left him there. After about fifteen minutes, the artist came and greeted his friend and led him to his studio to view the painting. The artist said, *"I suppose you thought it strange to be left alone in a dark room for so long."*

"Yes, I did," replied the curious visitor.

"Well," said the artist, *"I knew that if you came into my studio with the glare of the street in your eyes you could not appreciate the fine coloring of the picture. So I left you in the dark room until the glare had worn out of your eyes."*

God sometimes leaves us "in the dark" for periods of time to get the glare of impure "floaters" out of our spiritual eyes. If you are currently in the dark, be still. What He has to show you will be worth the wait!

53

But Jesus said to him, "No one, having put his hand to the plow, and looking back, is fit for the kingdom of God."
---Luke 9:62

When Cortez came to the "New World," he burned the ships in the harbor. He knew that this "New World" held blessings immeasurable, but he also knew of the hardships as well. Cortez was wise enough to know that conquerors cannot afford to be distracted. Distractions can be costly. They may even cost you your life and the lives of those around you. One distraction that Cortez eliminated was the means to return to the "Old World."

Paul gave a similar warning to Timothy: *"You therefore must endure hardship as a good soldier of Jesus Christ. No one engaged in warfare entangles himself with the affairs of this life, that he may please Him who enlisted him as a soldier"* (2 Tim. 2:3-4).

The mission to which God has called our church is to convert sinners into saints, and saints into soldiers for the glory of Christ. Soldiers are enlisted in case of war. God says that we *are* at war. *"For though we walk in the flesh, we do not war according to the flesh. For the weapons of our warfare are not carnal but mighty in God for pulling down strongholds"* (2 Cor. 10:3-4).

You and I were enlisted in God's army when we were saved. Sad to say, many have not even been through "boot camp" much less become soldiers in the war against satan, our enemy.

We are living in the days in which God promised to pour out His Spirit upon all flesh. All over the world, we are seeing droplets of His grace and mercy. The flood is coming... a flood of God's Spirit and a flood of evil. When the two collide, there will be war.

However, we have a promise from God. *"When the enemy comes in like a flood, the Spirit of the Lord will lift up a standard against him"* (Isaiah 59:19). Yes, there is a war going on, but God promised us that *"the gates of hell shall not prevail against His church"* (Matt. 16:18). Gates are for defensive purposes... to keep enemies out. We are the enemies of satan. His gates cannot keep us out, but

132

they will not succumb if we do not storm them. We are called to be on the offensive, not the defensive.

Satan's strategy is to keep enlistment in God's army to a minimum. For those who have signed up, he seeks to keep them in the "mess hall" rather than on the front lines. For those on the front lines, he entices them to hide in foxholes. But God is looking for a few good men and women, boys and girls, who will charge the gates of hell with reckless abandon.

Jesus came for one purpose: to destroy the works of the devil (I John 3:8). He completed that work on the cross. Now, he tells us to stand our ground and to rescue those who have been taken captive by the enemy.

You may look at the world and think that the devil is winning. All you see is crime, corruption, immorality, and sin. But God is on a recruitment campaign. *"For the eyes of the Lord run to and fro throughout the whole earth, to show Himself strong on behalf of those whose heart is loyal (wholly committed) to Him"* (2 Chron. 16:9).

God gives us a strategy. *"Submit to God. Resist the devil, and he will flee from you"* (James 4:7). *"And they overcame him (the devil) by the blood of the Lamb and by the Word of their testimony, and they did not love their lives to the death"* (Rev. 12:11).

Do you notice the key to victory in spiritual warfare? Submitting absolutely to His Lordship, loving Jesus more than anything, or anyone else in the world... even to the point of dying for the love of Jesus. That is the winning blow.

Do you feel God calling you to enlist in His army? Do you sense Him calling you into the Green Berets... the special forces unit? Maybe you joined the special forces at one time, but are now cowering in a foxhole because the fighting became too intense.

Well, let me tell you, Soldier, our Commander-in-Chief is still at the helm. He still loves you. He always will. He will stand with you... guide you... comfort you... bind up your wounds. He will never forsake you. He's already struck the winning blow at the cross. Now let's storm the gates of hell and take back what God says belongs to Him and to us.

Burn your boats! Don't let the devil tempt you with a life raft. He knows that when your boat sinks, he goes down with the ship. Bon voyage, slewfoot!

54

But the end of all things is at hand: be ye therefore sober, and watch unto prayer.

---I Peter 4:7 (KJV)

Last night a strange thing happened to me. I was awakened out of a deep sleep with the feeling that something was crawling up my arm. Instead of slapping it, I reached over and pinched it off. It felt like a bug of some kind. I threw it onto the floor and turned on the light. It was a spider about the size of a quarter.

After disposing of the creature and allowing my pulse to settle back down to normal, I began to ponder the marvelous implications of this rude awakening. I was immediately impressed with how fearfully and wonderfully we are made. Take the skin for instance. It is tough and durable, yet extremely sensitive. The nerves in my skin know when to send pain impulses to my brain when the pressure of a foreign object threatens the safety of the body. And yet, my skin is so sensitive that it can awaken me out of a deep sleep when a minuscule creature crawls up my arm. Is God awesome, or what?

As I began to praise the Lord in the night watches, I saw that there was a spiritual lesson in this event as well. All born again believers have a Spirit which protects us like the skin of our bodies. Our Spirit is the instrument through which God warns us, instructs us, and leads us. Like the skin, our Spirit informs us of changes in our spiritual environment. Our Spirit tells us when something is right or wrong... truth or error. Our Spirit is far more reliable than our soul. God speaks through our Spirit and satan speaks through our soul. That is why we are admonished to walk in the Spirit so that we do not fulfill the lust of the flesh (Galatians 5:16).

Whenever we begin to listen to our soul rather than our Spirit, we become deceived. Our Spirit becomes desensitized to God's voice. Sometimes diseases such as leprosy attack the nervous system of the physical body causing one to be unable to feel pain. Without pain, we are unaware of a threat to our physical body and thus allow the threat to continue and cause harm. With our Spirit desensitized, we are unable to sense the creeping creatures of doubt, unbelief and confusion that seek to destroy us.

What causes our Spirit to become desensitized? Sin, unbelief, doubt, fear, rebellion, independent spirit, unforgiveness, bitterness, ad infinitum. Sin always anesthetizes our spiritual sensitivity and leads us to rely upon our soul for the source of truth. Our soul is easily deceived as evidenced by the devil's temptation in the Garden of Eden. Our only hope of walking in victory is to keep our Spirit extremely sensitive to the Truth of God's Word.

We are living in the last days. God is pouring out His Spirit as He promised in Joel chapter 2. However, satan is intensifying his assault as well upon the souls of people... especially the mind and emotions. He tells people the same old story that he told Eve... *"You can be like God! Do your own thing! Do what you think is right!"*

Satan's deception is becoming so much more intense and subtle. He is lying so well that people believe his lie to be truth. It is a last days phenomenon. ***"Satan.... deceives those who are perishing because they refused to love the truth and so be saved. For this reason God sends them a powerful delusion so that they will believe the lie and so that all will be condemned who have not believed the truth but have delighted in wickedness"*** (2 Thessalonians 2:9-11). Jesus said in Matthew 24:24 that in the last days ***"false Christs and false prophets will appear and perform great signs and miracles to deceive even the elect--- if that were possible."***

Beloved, in these last days, we must shut down every leak and every pinhole which drains our faith and love for the truth, or else we will be deceived. Ask the Lord to show you where you are leaking. He will surely tell you. Then confess the leak as sin... repent... and hold fast to the Truth. Don't take anything for granted. Be radically obedient to the Truth. It's the only way we are going to survive.

If you refuse to walk steadfastly according to Truth, one night you won't wake up when the spider of destruction crawls up your arm. ***"Be sober, be vigilant, for your adversary, the devil walks around seeking whom he may***

devour" (I Peter 5:8). Don't let him sneak up on you! Wake up, Beloved!

55

Forgetting what is behind and straining toward what is ahead, I press on toward the goal to win the prize for which God has called me heavenward in Christ Jesus.
—Philippians 3:13-14

Ever been to the circus and seen the elephants tied to a little stake in the ground with a skinny old chain? Mind boggling, isn't it? That huge, powerful elephant held by a chain that he could snap in two with one quick jerk. Ever wonder why he does not break free? Well, when he was a little tike... oh, four or five hundred pounds.... he tried as hard as he could to break that chain. He could never do it.

One day, he decided that the chain was unbreakable and his belief system bought it. Although he grew big and strong, his belief system was stymied and never outgrew that false belief. Although the chain is no match for his great strength, he still believes that it is unbreakable. And so he stands majestically imprisoned... not by the chain, but by his belief system.

Fleas have a similar mind-set. When put into a jar,

they jump and hit their heads on the lid... over and over again. After a few hundred attempts and a headache to beat the band, the fleas give up trying to jump any higher. Even when the lid is removed, they will not jump out because they believe it's impossible. They will jump right to where the lid was but no higher. Thus, they are enslaved with the door wide opened.

It is sad to say, but many Christians are like that. We were told to have faith, but it was merely "faith in faith." We missed the fact the faith is no better than it's object. For the Chrisitian, that would be Jesus. So, we tried to have enough faith, but every attempt failed because we were trusting in the wrong thing. Then, as we grew to know that faith is only as good as its object, we still were bound by our past failures much like the elephant.

Beloved, when we were born again, we entered covenant with our Lord. We exchanged all our stuff for all His stuff. We laid our weapons down and let Him do the battling for us. We gave him power of attorney, and He gave us His Name. We gave Him our life that was dead in sin, and He gave us His resurrected Life. What a deal for us!

However, many of us are still strangers to the covenant of promise. We do not fathom the incredible power of covenant with the God of the universe. When we fail to understand the provisions of covenant, we become like the elephant who has tremendous power but is held in bondage by a meager chain. We get a "flea mentality" and fail to realize that we have power to jump way out of that jar. As a matter of fact, we have power to burst thru the lid!

One of satan's major schemes is to remind us of our past. God wants to remind us of who we are in Him and the destiny that He's placed within us. He reminds us of our true identity. We are not Clark Kent's. We are Supermen and

Superwomen in covenant with an Almighty God who loves us enough to die for us.

Beloved, it's time to break the chains of slavery with which Satan has bound us all these years. Invoke your covenant privilege. Rebuke those lying emotions... the fear, the frustration, the loneliness, the confusion. Speak into being what God says is your privilege and provision as His child of covenant.

Sweet liberty is only one tug... one leap away. Go for it, Beloved!

56

This is what the LORD says: "Stand at the crossroads and look; ask for the ancient paths, ask where the good way is, and walk in it, and you will find rest for your souls." But you said, "We will not walk in it."

---Jeremiah 6:16

On the way to the office one morning, I began to notice that almost everyone was wearing their seatbelts. I do not normally think about such things as that, but the Lord used the observation to drop a spiritual principle into my heart while sitting at the stoplight.

I remember when auto stores began selling lap seat belts before they ever thought about making it mandatory to wear them. Dad stocked them in the Western Auto, and they were our biggest dust collectors. Nobody bought seatbelts. They were a nuisance and wrinkled your clothes. Then after much testing and experimentation, it was concluded that seatbelts saved lives. One by one, states began to pass laws making it mandatory to wear seatbelts.

When the law was passed, people paid very little attention. Wearing seatbelts had not become a way of life for most drivers. When state troopers began fining people for not wearing seatbelts, the negative motivation for wearing seatbelts outweighed the positive motivation of saving lives. I began wearing seatbelts because I did not have $80 to pay the fine.

Now when I get into my car, the first thing I do is put on my seatbelt. I do not even think about it. It has become part of my routine... my ritual. I do not think about being fined, or saving my life. I just do it because it is the best thing for me to do. Most of us do not do the right things in the beginning because it is the right thing to do. We need to be motivated. Most of us respond better to negative motivation, because we hate pain more than we love pleasure.

When I was a child, I didn't play in the road, because I'd get my tail torn up if I did. It never occurred to me that playing in the road was hazardous to my health. Now that I am older, I appreciate my parents keeping me out of danger by whatever means it took to do so. They loved me. That's why they disciplined me. Ultimately, I came around to my parent's way of thinking. Today, I don't play in the road because it's not a good thing for me to do.

We live today in a world that's going haywire. We have babies having babies. Twenty-eight year old grandmothers. Babies being murdered in the womb. Kids carrying automatic weapons to school and killing kids. Mind-numbing drugs to get us through the day. Rat races. As many divorces in the church as in the world. Sex, lies and video tapes. No absolutes. No integrity. No loyalty. No respect for authority. Ad infinitum.

Since the shooting in Colorado, there have been more seminars on preventing violence than Carter has liver pills. The Word of God tells us exactly what to do. *"**Stand at the crossroads and look; ask for the ancient paths, ask where the good way is, and walk in it, and you will find rest for your souls**"* (Jeremiah 6:16). But the rest of the verse says, *"**We will not walk in it.**"* Man's heart was hard in Jeremiah's day. It has not become much softer over the years.

Our world is haywire because we have departed from the ancient paths... the OLAM in Hebrew. The way God set things up. The way they were supposed to be from eternity past. When you violate the principles which God established, things go drastically awry. Beloved, we must return to those ancient paths, or we will become hopelessly lost with no sense of purpose and destiny.

We must get back to the OLAM of husbands loving their wives like Christ loved the church. Wives must reverence their husbands. Children must honor their parents. Husbands and wives must keep their marriage covenant vows until they are parted by death. Churches need to be beacons of light, truth and grace. They must drop the plumb-line of God's Word and point to the ancient paths with boldness and conviction without compromise.

How do we turn things around and unravel the chaos? One person... one family... one home at a time. Beloved, we must lay a foundation for future generations so that they start out higher and go farther than we did. We must teach our children diligently the principles of God's

Word and model before them the absolute truth of God's unchanging OLAM.

Father God loves us so much. We may not understand why Father seems so harsh in His discipline, but one day we will. Just do what He tells you even if it's just to avoid the chastisement. His principles and instructions will still save your life regardless of your motivation for obeying them. One day you will see how faithful, loving, and patient He's been with you. You will understand why He does what He does. In the meantime, quit complaining. Buckle up and enjoy the ride.

57

Then the dragon was enraged at the woman and went off to make war against the rest of her offspring—those who obey God's commandments and hold to the testimony of Jesus.
                                                                                    ---Revelation 12:17

I am frugal. Not cheap. I am a good steward of my God-given financial resources. That's why we went out and bought a wrecked, inexpensive car. We saved a lot of money by buying a wreck and having it repaired. I call that good stewardship. Others very close to me say that I am so tight that I squeek when I walk. We'll let God be the judge of that. Talk about stewardship... not only did God provide us with a cheap (excuse me... *inexpensive*) car, He also gave me a wonderful illustration of His love and grace.

Our new car is a black 1997 Toyota Camry with only ten thousand miles. She is a great car. However, she came from an abusive, dysfunctional family. She ran into something which was not her fault. Her bumper, fenders and headlights were broken. That should have been the extent of her damage; however, she was owned by an unappreciative, self-centered tyrant. When the wreck occurred, the damage was not sufficient to warrant another new car. The bully owner kicked in her rear quarter panels and dented her roof to increase the damage assessment in order to get a new car from the insurance company. She was damaged goods, and he didn't want her any more.

My Black Beauty had cigarette burns on her upholstery and stains on her carpet. Her tires were worn out after only ten thousand miles. She had been treated very badly.

When we went to look at her at the car hospital, she looked pretty sad. When she thought we were going to buy her, you could just see her smiling thru all those bruises. We took her to a car doctor that we trusted, and he fixed her up as good as new. She is so happy now. She has an owner who loves and appreciates her. We change her oil and filter every three thousand miles. We drive her like we have some sense. We vacuum her carpet and shine her dash. She now rides through town with her head held high.

I believe she knows what kind of owner she has. We keep cars until the wheels fall off. We take care of them, and they take care of us. She doesn't have to worry that we will sell her to another mean bully who will abuse her. And she has responded with wonderful gas mileage. She plays great music for us when we drive her. She keeps us warm in the winter and cool in the summer. We have a wonderful relationship.

At one time, we were all like Black Beauty. We were brand new... filled with excitement and anticipation about life. Then because of sin, we were bought by a mean, ugly bully named satan. He abused us. He drove us hard. He wore us out physically, emotionally, and spiritually. He's the one who caused us to wreck.

He was nice to us while he was wooing us. He told us about all the nice places he wanted to take us. He promised high octane thrills and fulfillment, but He failed to keep his promises. He just drove us recklessly down some dark, dead end roads until he wrecked us. Then as if that were not enough, he kicked us when we were down. He told us how worthless we were and continued to de-value us.

One day, a Savior came. He looked us over from one end to the other. He said, **"My, my, you have been treated pretty rough, haven't you? Well, not to worry, I have come to redeem you... to buy you back. I have bought and paid for you with my very own blood. I'm going to make you brand new... even better than when you rolled off the assembly line. I love you very much. From now on, I will take care of you."**

Jesus came to us after we had wrecked and were all messed up. He bought us (and we weren't cheap) when no one else would even look at us. He saw what we would look like before He ever fixed us. He always sees us as we shall be... not as we are or have been. He is a wonderful Owner.

He will keep our oil changed, our tires rotated, and our spots cleaned. And we will keep that new car smell for eternity. We are beautiful to Him. It is a privilege to let Him drive, isn't it?

Why don't you let Him know how much you appreciate Him by cranking right up. Respond quickly to His slightest touch of your steering WILL. You can trust Him. He would never steer you wrong!

58

Follow my example, as I follow the example of Christ.
—I Corinthians 11:1

Young people need models, not critics. I believe that is what Paul meant when he said, **"Follow me as I follow Christ."** Today, we have so many authority figures telling us to do what they say, not what they do. How hypocritical is that? I remember hearing about a young boy asking his dad for a drink of beer. The dad replied, *"Son, that stuff is awful."*

The son asked, *"Dad, if it's awful, how come you're drinking it?"*

"It's not THAT awful," answered the dad.

What kind of message are we sending our next generation? *"Do what I say, not what I do. Do what you want, just don't get caught. Everything is relative. There are no absolutes. How can it be so wrong when it FEELS so right?"*

Today we are reaping the devastating results of that philosophical gobbledy gook. I went to court one day with

145

a friend. When I walked into the courtroom, I smelled demon puke. You could almost see the demons hanging onto people and vomiting all over them. The people there all looked like dying calves in a hail storm. Gloom, despair and agony. Their eyes were dark and lifeless. No life. No joy. No peace. Talk about depressing!

I sat next to a girl with black fishnet stockings. Her eyelids, nose, upper and lower lips, ears and neck were all pierced. My heart broke for her. God let me see into the darkness of her soul revealing to me a lonely, insecure, terribly frightened little girl with no hope of ever being free. I could see a little girl whom God had created in His own image who was never meant to walk in that darkness. Along the way, satan had ambushed her, lied to her, and defiled her soul. He used people whom God had ordained to bless her and to launch her toward her destiny as instruments of cursing rather than blessing. Demons of rejection and deception clung to her, vomiting upon her their putrid lies, pain and bitterness.

How different would this woman have been had her father loved on her... kissed her... held her... affirmed her? What if she had grown up with a dad who was a visual aid of Father God's love for His children. Do you think she would have been in that courtroom had her mom lovingly modeled before her the virtues of a godly woman? I don't think so.

In 24 hours, we remember only about 20% of what we heard. But we remember for a long time the things we see. Then, if we actually *do* the thing we heard and saw, we really come to understand the principle. We get an inner image of the concept. It's kind of like riding a bicycle. Hearing about it and watching someone ride does not get it done. Only by doing it... getting on and riding... does the

146

inner image and understanding come.

I believe that's what is wrong with the body of Christ today. Too many hearers of the Word and not enough doers. James 1:22 says that if you hear the Word and don't do it, then you deceive yourself. If I could describe our society in one word it would be *deceived*. Even the church is deceived. We think we can go to church, sing a few songs, hear the Word and that's all there is to being a Christian. Bullfeathers! We are called to BE the church, not go TO it.

Let's take an example. Husbands, what does it mean to love your Bride like Christ loves the church? Do you honor her? Do you open the car door for her? Do you help her with her coat and her chair at restaurants? Do you tell her everyday that you love her? Do you kiss her and hold her often? Do you look at her through eyes that say to her how blessed you are to have her as your Bride? Do you lay down your life, your desires, your agendas to serve and prosper her? If not, then you are merely a hearer of the Word and not a doer. Today would be a good day to start doing the Word.

Wives, do you reverence your husband? Do you hold his hand at Wal Mart? Do you obey him as your head as Christ is the head of the church? Do you esteem him in front of others? Do you serve him out of love and devotion? Do you delight in keeping a stress-free home for him to relax from the rigors of his work? If not, then you are a mere hearer as well. Don't wait on him. Be the first to out-serve your husband. Nobody loved and served better than Jesus. Walk in His steps and see if your husband doesn't follow.

Saints of God, are you walking in integrity? Do you give an honest day's work for an honest day's pay? Do you show kindness to everyone? Do you walk humbly before the Lord? Are you teachable when criticized? Do you enjoy life?

Those are things that bring great joy to Father God. Be a doer. It blesses His heart.

Beloved, is there any Word of God that you are not doing? Confess it as sin, repent, and start doing the Word. A world is looking for a visual aid for the Christian life. Model it. Don't just talk about it. Do it! There are a lot of little eyes looking at you to see what to do. There are a lot more little girls in fishnet stockings and holes all over their faces who are looking for someone to show them the love and grace of Christ, not just tell them about it. There comes a time when knowing what to do must be translated into doing what you know.

Keep following Him, Beloved, so that those who follow you will know what to do!

59

"Cast all your anxiety on Him because He cares for you."
---I Peter 5:7

Ever feel like the weight of the world is on your shoulders? You have *all* the responsibility and *no* control? Do you ever feel like throwing your hands in the air and giving up? Does griping and complaining weed out blessing and praising from your conversations? Do you ever wonder why God put you in such a fix?

If anyone ever understood all of that, Moses did. If you have nothing else to praise God for, you should praise Him for not choosing you to do Moses' job. Think about it...

Moses was responsible for three to three and a half million people. First of all, they had to be fed. Feeding that many people would require a lot of food. According to the Quartermaster General of the Army, it is reported that Moses would need 1,500 tons of food each and every day. Did you know that it would require two freight trains each one mile long to transport that much food? And they needed that much food *everyday*!

You must remember that they were out in the desert. They would need firewood to use in cooking the food. To cook for that many people would require 4,000 tons of wood and a few more freight trains each a mile long to supply their needs for just one day! I don't know much, but aren't trees scarce in the desert? And were they not wandering around out there for 40 years?!?!

Oh yes... they had to have water, too. If they only had enough to drink and wash a few dishes, it would take 11,000,000 gallons each day.

And another thing... they had to get across the Red Sea in one night! If they walked on a narrow path, double file, the line would be 800 miles long and would require 35 days and nights to get through. So there had to be space in the Red Sea at least 3 miles wide so that they could walk 5,000 abreast in order to cross over in just one night!

There was still another problem. Every time they camped at the end of each day, a campground two-thirds the size of the state of Rhode Island was required... a total of 750 square miles. Think of that! That much space for just one night of camping! And they had to move and set up camp every day for 40 years!

Do you think Moses figured all this out before he left Egypt? I doubt it very seriously. Take heart, Beloved, we have the same God who loved and took care of His children in the wilderness with far less resources than we have at our disposal. About all the Israelites had was God and each other. That's all we need, too.

Sometimes we think our problems are so big, but our God is bigger than all our problems. He is able to do exceedingly abundantly above all that we could ever ask or think. He is a great God!

When we team up with Him, He assumes responsibility for all our problems. Just cast your cares and worries upon Him. He cares for you more than you will ever be able to comprehend. He will provide for you in *your* wilderness as well. Don't just take it from me... ask Moses!

60

The fire shall try everyone's work of what sort it is. If anyone's work which he has built endures, he will receive a reward."

---I Corinthians 3:13-14

George W. Boschke was the famous engineer who always loved to tackle the monstrous, near-impossible projects no one else would dare to touch. He built the tremendous seawall in Galveston, Texas to protect that exposed city from the ravages of hurricanes which frequent the coast of Texas. He built it with a steadfast confidence that defied even the strongest of hurricanes.

After building the seawall, he left for Oregon to build a railroad in the wilderness of that state. While on that project, 40 miles from civilization, an exhausted messenger rode in and handed a telegram to Boschke's assistant. The message stated that the Galveston seawall had been swept away by a second furious hurricane. The assistant dreaded relaying the message to his mentor.

Boschke read the telegram and laughed. *"This telegram is a black lie. I built that wall to stand."* Then, he turned around and went back to work, whistling and smiling serenely to himself. Sure enough, the message turned out to be based on a false report.

Every person built upon the foundation of Christ and His truth will stand, come wind, flood, storm, or whatever. We have nothing to fear, for Christ is our Rock and our Salvation. So, the next time satan comes with news of disaster and catastrophe, give him Boschke's message: *"That's a black lie. I have built my life to stand on Christ."* Then, go on whistling while you work!

61

Jesus said, "I praise You, Father, Lord of heaven and earth, because you have hidden these things from the wise and learned, and revealed them to little children."
---Matthew 11:25

When Kia, was entering her sophomore year in high school, she was not a starter on the volleyball team. After a couple of scrimmages, Kia was playing behind a taller teammate. She didn't think her lack of height should affect her playing time. She was disappointed, but she also understood the sovereignty of the Lord. She knew He was always in control. She also knew that we should let our requests be made known.

One day, she went to talk to Coach Grayson. Kia believed she was good enough to play... short or tall. She gave her a proposition: *"If I can't do the job, I'll sit the bench and be the best bench-warmer in the whole world. All I ask is a chance to prove that I can play."* She figured that God would do whatever was best for her and bring Him glory. To her, it was a "win-win" situation.

To make a long story short, Kia started the next game

and was a starter for the rest of her career. But that's not the point of the story.

After Kia's first "start," she rode home with me. That's when God gave me a lesson from "the mouth of a babe."

She said, *"Daddy, I've learned something."*

"What have you learned, Baby Girl?"

She replied with wisdom beyond her years, *"As long as we want our way and not God's, we get frustrated. But when we give God what He wants, it frees Him up to give us what we want."*

It took me over forty years to even begin to learn that lesson, and here's Baby Girl putting it into practice at sixteen. Talk about humbling.

She's right, you know. We must come to the place where we say to God, *"Lord, I know you know what's best for me. I thankfully accept my lot in life...be that superstar or spectator... pain or pleasure... sensation or suffering."* Until we do, we will always be trying to control our own destiny. If God were to grant our request while we were still in our self-centered mode, we would never come to totally trust and depend upon Him.

When we tell Him that His glory is our main concern, it frees Father God up to give us what we desire. It allows Him to give us our desires because He knows that He has our heart. Once He has our heart, He knows that our way won't get in the way of His. It's kind of biblical. ***"But seek ye first the kingdom of God and His righteousness, and all these things will be added unto you"*** (Matthew 6:33).

Are things not going your way? Are you frustrated? Irritated? Life to others is a bowl of cherries, and for you it's the pits? Would you like to have it your way?

Let me give you the key to unlock the door to

contentment and fulfillment. It's found in I Thessalonians 5:18... *"Give thanks in all circumstances, for this is God's will for you in Christ Jesus."*

Before you start thinking I'm crazy, let me say that there is a difference between being "thankful" and "giving thanks." I'm *thankful* if you buy me a steak dinner, but I have to *give thanks* when I have a flat tire.

God knows about flat tires, irritations, and frustrations. When you thank God for all the negative stuff as well as the good stuff, you acknowledge His sovereignty. Circumstances may or may not change, but knowing that He is in control of it all changes the way you look at them. If He is in control, then you don't have to be. Being in control is a full-time job and very exhausting. Jesus is the only One who can handle the work load. He says, *"Come to Me, all you who are weary and burdened, and I will give you rest"* (Matthew 11:28).

Being a "bench warmer" is not all that bad. I've had days when I'd love to have a rest. How about you? Come on and have a seat. I'm sure He'll have us back in the game soon enough. In the meantime, "Go, God!"

62

Do not let any unwholesome talk come out of your mouths, but only what is helpful for building others up according to their needs, that it may benefit those who listen.

---Ephesians 4:29

Ken Venturi is a golf analyst for CBS. He won the U.S. Open in 1967 when the tournament was last held at the Congressional Club in Washington, D.C. When Venturi won the Open, the golfers were required to play two rounds (36 holes) on the last day. In sweltering heat, Venturi had to be treated for heat exhaustion several times during the final day. He staggered up the 18th hole dazed and exhausted. He said that he can't even remember playing the last few holes. It was an amazing feat of stamina, endurance and skill... the marks of a true champion.

In a TV interview at this year's Open on Father's Day, Venturi wept as he told the story of that momentous day. After winning the Open, his first thought was that finally he had done something that would make his father proud of him. Venturi had spent his entire life trying to please his father. Sadly, winning the Open was not enough.

Instead of congratulating his son on his victory, Venturi's dad told him that he would have to work even harder to show people that his victory was not a fluke. Winning the Open was not enough. The Open champion was crushed. He might have been on top of the golf world, but his spirit was in the pit. He would have gladly traded the Open trophy for his dad's approval.

One day, Venturi was diagnosed with a circulation problem in his hand. The condition was serious. The loss of his fingers was a possibility. Venturi believed that success in golf was his only means of securing his dad's approval. The diagnosis scared him to death. The fear of losing his fingers and his golf career paled in comparison to losing the hope of ever gaining his father's approval.

With fear and trembling, Venturi told his dad about the diagnosis. His dad's response set him free from all his fears. His dad told him, *"Son, it doesn't matter if you lose your fingers or not. You are the best I ever saw."*

With those words, Venturi's life changed. He's never been the same. He went back to the doctor and told him to do whatever he needed to do. Venturi was at peace.

It would boggle your mind to know how many men have never heard a single word of encouragement from their dads. That's why so many men are climbing the corporate ladder only to find upon reaching the top that it was leaning against the wrong wall. They really weren't looking for fame, fortune, and notoriety. They just wanted to do something that would make dad proud.

Words. Mere words. Do you see how powerful words can be? A U.S. Open champion would give up his trophy and even his fingers for one, *"Well done, son."*

What keeps us from giving those life-giving words to those we love? Could it be that the deprivation of those words in our own lives have wounded us so deeply that we can't utter them ourselves? Let me tell you something. You have a heavenly Father Who is bursting with pride over you. I'll bet he even pulls out his wallet and flashes your picture to all the angels. I can hear Him saying now, **"That's my boy! That's my girl! Isn't he/she something?"**

I don't care if you are an Open champion or a hacker who can't break a hundred, your Heavenly Father thinks you're the best He ever saw.

63

"For My thoughts are not your thoughts, neither are your ways My ways" declares the Lord.

---Isaiah 55:8

I have often pondered the fact that the game of golf and the Christian life are so very similar. For instance, golf is a game of opposites. To make the ball go up, you hit down. To make the ball go down, you swing up. To make the ball go left, you swing to the right. To make the ball go right, you swing to the left. No wonder golf is such a frustrating game.

There is nothing natural about golf. Someone who has never swung a golf club will do everything contrary to a good, sound golf swing. To develop a good golf swing requires training the mind and muscles to function in ways contrary to our natural tendencies. A good swing is most unnatural.

157

The same is true with our Christian life. Our natural tendency when offended is to punch people's lights out. God says to love your enemies and do good to them that hate you. How unnatural is that? God says that we are not to return evil for evil, but to return good for evil.

A.W. Tozer best describes what I mean: *"A real Christian is an odd number. He feels supreme love for One Whom he has never seen, talks familiarly everyday to Someone he cannot see, expects to go to heaven on the virtue of Another, empties himself in order to be full, admits he is wrong so he can be right, goes down in order to get up, is strongest when he is weakest, richest when he is poorest, and happiest when he feels worst. He dies so he can live, forsakes in order to have, gives away so he can keep, sees the invisible, hears the inaudible, and knows that which passeth knowledge."*

All our natural tendencies come from our fallen nature and the world's system which are totally contrary to God's ways. That's why God's Word admonishes us... **"do not be conformed to this world but be transformed by the renewing of our minds so that we may know what is the good, perfect, and acceptable will of God"** (Romans 12:2). Just as we must overcome our natural inclinations in order to develop a good golf swing, we must re-train our minds according to God's Word if our Christian life is to ever become "natural."

Unlike learning to play golf, we have the Master Teacher, the Holy Spirit, Who lives within us and constantly gives us tips. As a matter of fact, He makes the fundamentals become natural. Here's what He does: **"I will put My laws in their hearts, and I will write them on their minds"** (Hebrews 10:16). **Then He adds, "Their sins and lawless acts I will remember no more."**

Don't you wish the game of golf was like that? It's not. You pay a severe penalty for hitting the ball out of bounds. God, on the other hand, forgives your bad shots so you can still shoot par. Jesus has already parred the course for you.

So, why not tee up your day and swing away. Quit worrying about sand traps that look like the Sahara and water holes that resemble the Atlantic. Jesus survived the desert, and He can walk on water. Enjoy your round!

64

When men fall down, do they not get up? When a man turns away, does he not return?

---Jeremiah 8:4

Y ou'll never make it to the Baseball Hall of Fame without making a few outs. Even God's greatest heroes who made it to The Hall of Faith in Hebrews chapter 11 were far from perfect. To be a hero, you have to take some risks. Failure is never final. Failure only comes when you refuse to get up and keep going. As a matter of fact, most of our real wisdom comes from the lessons we learn from our mistakes.

Many of baseball's Hall of Famers held both good and not so good records. Take a look:
- ▸ **Babe Ruth** held the homerun record of 714 homers for 39

years. But did you know that he struck out 1,330 times? A major league record until it was broken by another Hall of Famer.

▸ **Ty Cobb** stole more bases than anyone until 1982. He was the King of Thieves when it came to stealing bases. But did you know that he holds the record for being thrown out the most times trying to steal in a season... 38?

▸ **Hank Aaron** broke Ruth's homerun record with 755 homeruns. But did you know he holds the record for hitting into the most double plays?

▸ **Reggie Jackson** was called "Mr. October" because of his superlative play in the World Series. But did you know that he was the first major league player to strike out 2,000 times?

Earl Weaver, former manager of the Baltimore Orioles, once said: *"Managers are always learning, mostly from our mistakes. That's why I keep a list of my mistakes at home for reference. I used to carry the list around in my pants pocket, but I finally had to stop. It gave me a limp."*

Aren't you glad that our Lord Jesus doesn't give up on us when we make a few mistakes. He never reviles us, or chides us, but pulls for us, always reaching out His hand to pick us up when we fall. Remember the woman caught in adultery? **"Neither do I condemn you,"** Jesus said. **"Now go and sin no more."** Remember Peter denying that He even knew the Lord? When Jesus rose from the tomb, he told the ladies, **"Go tell the disciples... and especially Peter... that I am alive. He's got another chance."**

Beloved, we belong to the God of a "second chance." You have to swing to hit a homerun. So what if you miss it a few times. You'll never hit it out of the park unless you take a big swing at it. Don't sit there paralyzed, afraid of failing. Heroes of the faith are risk-takers. They know that if they strike out, they will get another turn at bat. You can't make a mistake with a sincere heart. He loves us as much when we drag the bat back to the dugout after striking out as He does when we trot home after hitting it out of the park.

So, go for it, Beloved. Don't stand there with the bat on your shoulder. Swing for the fence! Keep swinging, Slugger, and one of these days... POW! There's a drive! Way back! That ball is going... going... GONE! It's outta here!

And one day... so will we!

65

He came to a broom tree, sat down under it and prayed that he might die.

---I Kings 19:4

Ever been to the broom tree? Sooner or later, if you walk with God, you will visit the broom tree. The broom tree is not for the wimps who can't cut it like some Pharisees would have you believe. Warriors sit under broom trees, too.

The warrior in this passage is none other than Elijah, the great prophet of God. All who walk with God become weary at times, especially after great triumphs. Elijah had just experienced his greatest victory in the Lord. He had stood before four hundred and fifty prophets of Baal, and

God had zapped them.

However, we are never more vulnerable to attack than after a great victory. We tend to let our guard down and bask in the glory. That is when the enemy attacks. In this case, he used Jezebel. *"May the gods deal with me ever so severely, if by this time tomorrow I do not make your life (Elijah) like that of one of them (prophets of Baal)"* (I Kings 19:2).

On the surface, it seemed but a trifle. A man of God calling down fire from heaven and killing 450 false prophets in a day being driven over the edge by the threat of one measley woman? It happens. But why?

Ever heard the saying, *"Fatigue makes cowards of us all"*? Take a look at verse 5: *"Then he lay down under the tree and fell asleep."* Elijah was tired. He should have been. It takes a lot of energy to kill 450 false prophets in a day.

One of the pitfalls of walking with God is the feeling of invincibility that comes with it. Sometimes one does not think he needs rest or restoration. He goes on and on without ever stopping to sharpen his axe. When he runs into a minor thorn, his axe is so dull that he can't chop it down even though he has just felled a huge tree.

How does God deal with tired, depressed prophets? For one thing, He understands. Believe me. *He knows our frame. He remembers that we are dust* (Psalm 103:14). God sent an angel to Elijah. The angel gently woke him up and gave him something to eat. He ate and drank. He lay down and slept some more. Elijah was really tired. God knew what he needed.

God sent the angel a second time. The angel told Elijah to get up and eat because the journey was much too hard for him. When walking with God, He sometimes sends circumstances to destroy our sense of invincibility.

Cockiness in the spirit can get you killed. God is good to remove that pride before it has a chance to destroy us.

Elijah got the message. He knew he must meet God. So he traveled forty days and nights to Horeb, the mountain of God. When he got there, he was still depressed. He was still partying... pity-partying, that is.

God used one of His patented questions to get Elijah to take a look at himself. *"What are you doing here, Elijah?"* (vs. 9).

Elijah replied, *"I have been very zealous for the Lord God Almighty. The Israelites have rejected your covenant, broken down your altars, and put your prophets to death with the sword. I am the only one left, and now they are trying to kill me, too"* (vs. 10).

Isn't he pitiful? Don't look so spiritual. You and I have said the same thing. Elijah looked for God to vote for him, and God doesn't vote. God heals and restores. Sympathy keeps us sick.

God then told Elijah to go out and stand on the mountain in the presence of the Lord. There was a great wind, a great earthquake, and a great fire, but God was not in any of those. After these things, there came a gentle whisper.

Many times we miss the still, small voice of God because we are looking for Him in the wind, earthquakes, and fire. To hear God is our greatest need... especially when we are down and out. It is essential to be still if we are to hear His voice.

God asked Elijah a second time: *"What are you doing here, Elijah?"* Elijah gave God the same song and dance as he did before. *"I am the only one left trying to do your will. Woe is me"* (vs. 14).

Still in the throes of self-pity, the Lord outlined for

163

Elijah a pathway out of the wilderness. It will work for us as well. Let's take a look:

First, God told him to go back the way he came. When we get down, we lose sight of our purpose and meaning in life. We need to go back and remember the last thing God told us to do and start doing that again. When we get depressed, we give up on the fundamentals... Bible reading, prayer, and time alone with God. That's why we get tired and down to begin with. We start taking God for granted. Get back to basics!

Secondly, God gave him some goals. Goal-oriented people are seldom depressed. Elijah's goal was accomplished when Baal's prophets were destroyed. There is a natural let down after a big goal is achieved. That's why we need new ones. God created us to be goal-oriented. Without a vision, the people perish. Elijah's new assignment was to anoint three people: two kings, Hazael and Jehu, and a prophet as his successor, Elisha.

Thirdly, God gave Elijah some help and protection. God said that Jehu would kill any enemy that escaped Hazael, and Elisha would get what Jehu missed. We all need garden friends. Jesus needed Peter, James, and John to pray for Him in the garden. We need those kind of friends as well. Seek them out. Ask them to pray for you. You need them. They are not a luxury. They are a necessity.

Finally, God gave Elijah hope. *"Hope deferred makes the heart sick"* (Proverbs 13:12). God assured Elijah that he was not alone. God had 7,000 of His own children who had not bowed to Baal. When we sit beneath our broom tree, what we need is hope. It's hard to have faith without hope. But as much as we need faith and hope, what we need more than anything else is love.

When God found Elijah under the broom tree, He did

not preach to him. He loved him. Find a broom tree today and see if you can sweep someone out with His love. Unless, of course, you are sitting there yourself. In that case, enjoy the shade and the rest. It won't be long before you, just like Elijah, will be swept away by His love.

66

"There is not another jar left." Then the oil stopped flowing.
—2 Kings 4:6

There was a widow in 2 Kings chapter 4 that was destitute and on the verge of losing everything she owned to creditors. They even threatened to take her two sons as slaves in order to pay the debt. She cried out to Elisha for help. Upon his arrival, he asked her what she had left in her house. She told him that all she had left was a little bit of oil.

Elisha told her to go to all her neighbors and collect as many empty bottles as she could. He then instructed her to go into her house and shut the door behind her. Along with her sons, she was to take that little bit of oil and fill the empty jars. When the last jar was filled, the oil stopped flowing. Elisha told her to go sell the oil, pay off her creditors and live on what was left.

What a story! Isn't it interesting that the oil kept flowing as long as there were empty jars? Which brings us to the question... *"Has the oil stopped flowing in your life? Has the oil of God's Spirit been quenched because you have run out of empty jars?"*

I believe God had that widow right where He wants you and me. All she had was a "little" oil. When we are empty, God is able to fill us with the oil of His Spirit so that our lives are fruitful and glorifying to Him. But He must have *empty* jars.

We may have plenty of jars, but they are filled with things that leave no room for God. I'm not saying those things are bad. Many of the things in our jars are very good. Nevertheless, the jars must be absolutely empty to keep the oil flowing. What kind of things are filling the jars of your life today?

The widow could have been rich had she continued collecting empty jars. Are you living on poverty level spiritually because you have run out of empty jars? The problem is not a shortage of oil... but a shortage of empty vessels. Quick! Hand me another jar!

67

We receive from Him whatever we ask, because we [watchfully] obey His orders [observe His suggestions and injunctions, follow His plan for us] and [habitually] practice what is pleasing to Him. And this is His order (His command, His injunction): that we should believe in (put our faith and trust in and adhere to and rely on) the name of His Son Jesus Christ (the Messiah), and that we should love one another, just as He has commanded us.

---I John 3:22-23 (AMP)

One Sunday morning a man was awakened by his lovely bride and told that it was time to get ready for church. The man groaned and said, *"I don't want to go to church. The church is cold and dead. The people are mean and hateful. And I don't get a thing out of it."*

To that the wife replied, *"Honey, you have to go. You're the pastor!"*

A few years ago, that was me. It was during this leg of my wilderness journey that a fine young man named Billy Griffin called and asked me to take part in his ordination service as he entered the pastorate. I accepted the invitation but I would have rather been beaten with a whip.

I told Wanda on the way to the church that Sunday

167

evening that I felt like an orange that had every drop of juiced squeezed out of it. And here I was being squeezed again. I wanted to leave the ministry and start digging ditches for a living. Now I was supposed to go and encourage Billy to "give'em heaven." I was lower than a snake's belly in a wagon rut.

Somehow, I got through the service. Billy was more of an encouragement to me than I was to him. That's when I met the coolest, most refreshing waterhole I'd ever seen.

His name was Ernest Maley. I'll never forget him. After everyone had left the auditorium for the reception hall, I saw this tall, gray-haired man walking down the aisle to meet me. For all I know, he could have been an angel. I do know the message he had for me was angelic.

He stuck out his hand and said, *"Kenny, you're a man of God. God told me to tell you that He was not finished with you yet. He has His hand on you and has great plans for you. Don't you give up."*

I didn't know this man from Adam, but I was strangely drawn to him. He had a calm... a peace about him that was so soothing. Then he said, *"Kenny, do you know how good God is?"*

I said, *"No, Ernest, right now I don't. But I'm sure you are going to tell me."*

He then pulled a cassette tape out of his pocket and handed it to me. *"This is my testimony. Do you see this finger?"* He held up his hand revealing the index finger missing at the knuckle. He continued his story... *"I'm just a poor ditch digger* (He really owned a construction company.). *One day, we were laying concrete when I cut my finger off. The first thing the Lord reminded me of was Romans 8:28... 'All things work together for good to them that love God.'"*

"Well, I was bleeding like a stuck pig all over the place. I didn't have a handkerchief or nothing. Do you know how good God is? Let me tell you. We had gone to MacDonald's for lunch, and God had left a big wad of napkins in the seat of my truck! Is God good or what?"

I stood there in a waterhole of my own... tears of conviction. Here I was griping and complaining about how bad God, people and the world in general were treating me, and this man was praising God for a wad of MacDonald's napkins to hold his bleeding, chopped-off finger. I stood there and wept like a baby.

Ernest went on to tell me that he drove himself to the hospital and witnessed to six people including the nurse in the emergency room. He gave away six of his testimony tapes and six Bibles while he was there. That's Ernest's ministry... sharing his testimony and giving away the Bible on cassette tapes. Amazing!

I had to ask, *"Ernest, how did you get this way?"*

"This way, what?"

"This attitude of gratitude. This peace. This joy. This love of Jesus. How did you get it?" I had to know.

Ernest smiled and began his story. *"Years ago I was sitting in church one Sunday night. I'd always gone to church, but I didn't know a thing about God. The Lord spoke to me that night."*

"Ernest, you don't know me, do you?"

I said, *"No, Lord, I really don't."*

"Do you want to know Me, Ernest?

"Oh, yes, Lord. I do. I really do."

"Then I want you to take me seriously, Ernest. Take Me at My Word. Don't question it. Just do it. Do that, and I will become more real to you than you can ever imagine."

169

"I did what He said, and ever since then He has been so real... Do you know how good God is?" he asked with tears welling up in his eyes.

Then the Lord began speaking to me. **"Kenny, you know the difference between you and Ernest? You take me *literally*. You quote My Word and you will argue and defend it against anyone who would dare to deny its truth. But Ernest takes me *seriously*. He doesn't just quote it... he does it! You quote, *'In everything give thanks.'* Ernest thanks me. That's the difference."**

"Do you want Me to be real to you like I am to Ernest?"

"Oh, yes, Lord. I do."

"Then take Me seriously. Just do it."

I did take Him seriously that night. I promised the Lord that I would be a "doer" of the Word from that point on. You know what? God and Ernest were both right. I've never been the same since that night.

Do you know how good God is?

P.S. Two months after I met Ernest, he died. He always said that he wanted to go home to be with the Lord after he had worked at least a good half a day. One day after pouring concrete all morning, Ernest went home to be with the Lord right after lunch. I wouldn't be surprised to find that he had gone to MacDonald's.

Now I never wipe my mouth with a MacDonald's napkin without thinking about how good God is! If it worked for Ernest and me, I'll bet it will work for you. Get serious and see!

68

For the LORD loves the just and will not forsake his faithful ones.

----Psalm 37:28

I saw a bumper sticker one time that described me perfectly. It said: *"I'm a very responsible person. If anything goes wrong... I'm responsible."* I used to believe that God held me responsible for the attitudes and actions of everyone in the world. Talk about "stinking thinking." Father kept telling me that I was only responsible for what He told me to do and say. What people did after that was between them and Him. Somehow I could never get that message to drop from my head to my heart.

Then one day, I heard this story. I don't even know who told it, but when I heard it, the light came on and my self-imposed burden was lifted. I hope this waterhole quenches your thirst for freedom from "hyper-responsibility."

There was a man who was asleep one night in his cabin when suddenly his room filled with light and the Savior appeared. The Lord told the man He had a work for him to do, and showed him a large rock in front of his cabin. The Lord explained that the man was to push against the

171

rock with all his might. This the man did... day after day. For many years he toiled from sun up to sun down, his shoulders set squarely against the cold, massive surface of the unmoving rock pushing with all his might. Each night the man returned to his cabin sore and worn out, feeling that his whole day had been spent in vain.

Seeing that the man was showing signs of discouragement, satan decided to enter the picture placing thoughts into the man's mind such as: *"You have been pushing against that rock for a long time, and it hasn't budged. Why kill yourself over this, you are never going to move it?"* Thus, he gave the man the impression that the task was impossible and that he was a failure.

These thoughts discouraged and disheartened the man even more. *"Why kill myself over this?"* he thought. *"I'll just put in my time, giving just the minimum effort and that will be good enough."* And that he planned to do until one day he decided to make it a matter of prayer and take his troubled thoughts to the Lord. *"Lord,"* he said, *"I have labored long and hard in your service, putting all my strength to do that which you have asked. Yet after all this time, I have not even budged that rock a half a millimeter. What is wrong? Why am I failing?"*

The Lord responded compassionately, **"My child, when long ago I asked you to serve Me and you accepted, I told you that your task was to push against the rock with all your strength, which you have done. Never once did I mention to you that I expected you to move it. Your task was to push. And now you come to Me, your strength spent, thinking that you have failed. But is that really so? Look at yourself. Your arms are strong and muscled, your back sinewed and brown, your hands calloused from constant pressure, and your legs have**

172

become massive and hard. Through opposition you have grown much and your abilities now surpass that which you used to have. Yet you haven't moved the rock. But your calling was to be obedient and to push and to exercise your faith and trust in My wisdom. This you have done. Now, my child, I WILL MOVE THE ROCK!"
(author unknown)

I asked the Lord one day, "*Lord, how could you ever be happy and enjoy life? You had the weight of the entire world on your shoulders. A lot of the people You created would not believe in you. They were doomed to be separated from you for eternity. I have a small church to tend, and I worry about them all the time. What's your secret?*"

The Lord said to me, **"Kenny, you are assuming responsibility that doesn't belong to you. While I was here, I was only responsible to say what I heard Father say and do what I saw Him doing. When I died on the cross, it was finished... everything that Father had sent Me to do. That's your *only* responsibility as well. I'll take care of MY sheep. They don't belong to you. I'm just allowing you to feed and tend them for Me. Now relax. They will be just fine. And so will you."**

69

For me to live is Christ...

—Philippians 1:21

When we get to heaven, there are going to be more "unsaved" people there than "saved" people. Now that I have your attention, let me explain. In Matthew 1:21, the angel told Joseph that Jesus would "*save His people from their sins.*" Salvation is not merely going to heaven when we die. Salvation means to be "*saved from the bondage of sin right now...today.*"

In order to go to heaven, Jesus said, we must "be born again." That second birth gets us to heaven. But Jesus is able to do "***exceeding abundantly above all that we could ever ask or think according to His power that works within us***" (Ephesians 3:20). God really, really loves us. "***For if, when we were God's enemies, we were reconciled to Him through the death of His Son, how much more, having been reconciled, shall we be saved through His life!***" (Romans 5:10). Saved from what? The power and bondage of sin!

Most saints are "unbelieving believers." They know enough to get to heaven through the new birth, but they have never believed in the Lord Jesus with their whole

174

being. They have never taken Him seriously. Never been radically obedient.

Let me ask you a question. Are you saved? Before you answer, let me tell you that Christ has accomplished three things for us. First, through faith in Him we can be born again. Second, through His blood we can be forgiven. Third, through His life we can be saved. Do you realize that you can possess the first two and never participate in the third?

Countless numbers of Christians are truly born again and yet live in constant defeat and bondage to sin, guilt, anxiety, doubt and worry. Let me illustrate with a fish story. One day, a young fish said to an old fish, "*I long someday to see the great ocean.*"

The old fish said with a look of amazement, "*Son, you are IN the great ocean!*"

The young fish replied, "*What? I don't see any great ocean.*"

The young fish failed to see the great ocean because he had preconceived notions of what it looked like. Many Christians miss the abundant life for the same reason. Christianity is not a set of rules, or a doctrine, or a "way" of life. Christianity IS life. The Life of Christ lives within us.

Christian growth is not attaining what we do not have. It is simply becoming aware of what we've always had since the day we were saved... the very Life of Jesus. "**For me to live is Christ...**" (Philippians 1:21).

Are you tired of trying to measure up to unattainable standards? Jesus invites you to take a rest... on Him! Who knows, maybe you'll be one of the "saved" who makes it to heaven.

70

Do nothing out of selfish ambition or vain conceit, but in humility consider others better than yourselves.
---Philippians 2:3

One Saturday morning while channel surfing and waiting for the ball game to come on, I ran across this talk show. I heard this woman say, *"If you are out there and thinking of filing for divorce, don't do it. Give my program 24 hours, and you'll be packing for a second honeymoon."*

Well, this lady had piqued my interest. I kept listening. Although she never mentioned anything about biblical principles or about being a Christian, her principles were right out of the Bible. Her statements just confirmed what God has said all along. Biblical principles will always work regardless of who implements them...Christians or non-believers.

The host asked her, *"Why do people get married, and why do they divorce?"*

Her answer came right out of the pages of Scripture even though she didn't admit it. She said, *"A man falls in love with and marries a woman who makes him feel good about himself when he is with her."*

That makes sense to me. We all want to be around people who make us think well of ourselves... believe in ourselves... feel good about ourselves. That's why Jesus was so popular with the wilderness wanderers. He loved them just the way they were. There were no strings attached to His acceptance and love. He just loved them and always brought out the best in them. Jesus was One of whom you could say, *"I feel best about me when I'm around you."*

She went on to say that a man does not have an affair because he falls in love with or is physically attracted to another woman. He's attracted to another woman because she makes him feel better about himself than his wife does. Interesting, isn't it?

God created us with needs before The Fall. God created us needy so that we would depend upon Him. God hates *independence*. When we have an unmet need, it prompts us to go to the supply to have that need met. God said that **"He would supply all our needs according to His riches in glory by Christ Jesus"** (Philippians 4:19). God has the solution before we ever know we have a problem. Needs are simply the "prompters" that signal us to run to the Supply.

However, since The Fall, we have had a tendency to meet those needs selfishly, or in our own way. Larry Crabb says that we are all ticks looking for a dog. Many times when two people get married, one expects the other to meet his/her needs. But to the surprise of both, they find that they are simply two ticks with no dog. Hence, needs go unmet, and the search continues for someone or something to meet those needs.

Jesus gave us the supreme example of how to handle unmet needs. He said that it is better to give than to receive. The Bible says that **"each of you should look not only to**

177

your own interests, but also to the interests of others" (Philippians 2:4). God's way to success is to make others successful. We get lifted up when we lift up others.

Have you ever helped someone out and received the greater blessing? See! It's the way God made us. We were created to be lovers... lovers of God and lovers of people. God is a relational God. Jesus said that the greatest commandment is to love God will all our heart, mind, soul, and strength, and to love our neighbor as ourselves. He is a God of love. And we are made in His image.

God's love means giving of yourself sacrificially to meet the needs of another not expecting anything in return. Do you love that way? Do you think it would make a difference in your relationships if you did?

Now I know what you are thinking. *"I have needs, too. Nobody cares about my needs."* As long as you insist on being a tick, you will never be satisfied. Try meeting the needs of your spice (spouses are the "spice" of life), your children, your family, your friends, and see if your needs are not met in the meantime.

Ask Jesus to love them through you. Ask Him to let you see the real needs of those around you. Then ask Him for the grace to meet those needs in His Name. You may be packing up for a second honeymoon yourself!

71

But we have this treasure in jars of clay to show that this all-surpassing power is from God and not from us.

---2 Corinthians 4:7

Jesus is the Way, the Truth, and the Life. He is our "All-in All." Paul said, *"For me to live is Christ"* (Philippians 1:21).Is that true for you as well?

Jesus is the only One Who brings order out of chaos... strength out of weakness... joy out of sorrow... beauty out of ashes. He died that He might be our Life. We were *"dead in trespasses and sins"* (Ephesians 2:1) and Jesus gave us His life.

Our commitment to Jesus can be no greater than our revelation of Who He is and what He has done for us. Our revelation of Him can be no greater than our obedience to Him. Our obedience to Him can be no greater than our trust in Him. Our trust can be no greater than our knowledge of Him. Do you see how our whole existence hinges on our *knowing* Him?

How do we get to know Him? Paul explains that in 2 Corinthians 4:8ff... *"We are hard pressed on every side, but not crushed; perplexed, but not in despair; persecuted, but not abandoned; struck down, but not* *destroyed. **We always carry around in our body the death of Jesus, so that the life of Jesus may also be revealed in our body. For we who are alive are always being given over to death for Jesus' sake, so that His life may be revealed in our mortal body. So then, death is at work in us, but life is at work in you.***"

Do you see that? As we enter the death of Christ, Jesus lives. Is that not our goal? Do we not desire and long for Jesus to live fully and freely in us? But the flesh dies very reluctantly. That is why God graciously allows tribulation. Acts 14:22 tells us that *"we must through much tribulation enter the kingdom of God."* The Kingdom of God is simply anywhere that Jesus is King and Lord and where His subjects are in absolute submission to Him. If you are obeying the Lord, then you are in the Kingdom of God.

How did you learn obedience? Probably like Jesus Who learned obedience through the things that He suffered. But unlike Jesus, much of our tribulation is brought on by our own unbelief and disobedience. God patiently waits on us until we come to the place that we realize our misery has been our own fault. When we become afraid to think or act apart from His leading and will wait on Him and obey when He responds to us, then we truly enter the kingdom of God. We enter His *rest*.

Are you tired of trying to be good enough? Tired of struggling to please both God and man? Are you ready for some rest? Then come to Jesus, and He will give you rest. Quit griping about all the distresses, necessities, discouragements, and persecutions and start glorying in them. They are the very means by which God is escorting you into His kingdom and into His rest.

When you let go, you will find that He is there to catch you. He will never let you fall. And when you are in His hands, He will fashion you into a vessel of honor, sanctified and suitable for His use.

Did you know that the only difference between a clay pot and a fine, expensive crystal vase is the amount of heat applied during the curing process? The crystal vase must be cured at a much greater temperature than a clay pot. But isn't that vase beautiful when it comes out of the fire? How clear and transparent it is! Its beauty quickly dispels the memory of the fire.

How about you, clay pot? Is Jesus worth a little extra heat to make you a vessel so transparent that nothing hinders the view of the Master within you?

Peter was a clay pot when he asked Jesus what he would get out of leaving his home and livelihood to follow Him. After Peter had traversed the curing fires of tribulation, he said to the lame beggar at the Temple, *"Silver and gold have I none, but such as I have, give I unto thee..."*(Acts 3:6 KJV). The fire had transformed Peter from a *getter* into a *giver*. The fire had made him so crystal clear that the very Life of Jesus shined through him.

"Beloved, think it not strange concerning the fiery trial which is to try you, as though some strange thing happened unto you: But rejoice, inasmuch as ye are partakers of Christ's sufferings; that, when his glory shall be revealed, ye may be glad also with exceeding joy" (I Peter 4:12-13 KJV).

Peter rejoiced in his trials, and it *crystallized* him. Start rejoicing in yours today and see if your view of Jesus does not become *crystal clear!*

72

"The refining pot is for silver and the furnace for gold, but the Lord tests the hearts."

---Proverbs 17:3

Boy, does He test hearts! I have never seen times like these in all my life. Today, commitment is almost an extinct species. Contract marriages in which couples pledge their loyalty to one another *until* one becomes fat or bald are becoming the norm. Whatever happened to faithfulness, dependability, and loyalty? Businesses worship the almighty dollar, and people are as expendable as a watermelon seed. We use people and love things in our culture. We move from experience to experience never stopping to ponder where our path may lead us eternally.

God has allowed mankind to have his way. Every man seems to do what is right in his own eyes. Throughout Scripture, the people whom God judged were first allowed to go blind (spiritually). Is that not scary? You do not have to be a rocket scientist to see how blind our society is becoming. Open, unabashed sexual perversion...R-rated T.V. programs in prime time... abortion on demand for any reason... political corruption... greed... selfishness... I could go on forever.

What is God doing about all this? I believe that He is turning up the heat. God's children are being cast into the refining pot and into the furnace. Many are in the refining fires of tough job situations, abused by a value system based on greed and "bottom lines" rather than serving the needs of consumers. Still others are in the melting pot of ill health, experiencing the hopelessness of deteriorating physical conditions that never seem to get any better. Others are feeling the heat of strained marriages, bombarded by a world system that demands us to live up to standards and time constraints that God never intended for us.

I see more people at the end of their ropes than ever before. I believe God is using the furnace of affliction to burn away the dross of our independent spirits. Jesus wants to be our very Life...our Hope...our reason for living. As He turns up the heat, the dross of selfishness and sin rise to the top. That's when He reaches down with his spatula of grace and scrapes the dross away.

The old goldsmith used to say that he could tell the gold was pure when he could see his reflection on the surface. How do we know when we have been purified? When Jesus looks at us and sees His reflection.

I know it gets hot, Beloved, but remember this: On the day when Jesus looks at you and sees His reflection, the smile on His face will be worth it all! Keep shining!

73

Call to me and I will answer you and tell you great and unsearchable things you do not know.

—Jeremiah 33:3

Pastor Tim Gaud was doing rather well on the west coast. His church in Tacoma, Washington was growing and the services were being televised rather extensively throughout the northwest. But alas, as with most ministers worth their salt, Tim became overwhelmed by the tremendous needs on every hand. He worked day and night with seemingly little fruit to show for it. In the eyes of the world, He was the consummate TV minister, but to Tim... Well, he thought God had forgotten all about him.

Having slid off into the "Slough of Despond," Tim decided to leave his west coast ministry and start anew in the east. He loaded his family and all their earthly belongings up and headed east, not knowing where he was going.

Along the way, they stopped at a fast-food restaurant to eat lunch somewhere in Ohio. While his wife and kids ate their burgers, Tim took a walk pondering where God was in all of this. He happened by a telephone booth. Suddenly, the phone began to ring. Looking around for someone expecting a call and finding none, he sauntered over and picked up the receiver.

"*Hello,*" Tim answered.

"*Phone call for Pastor Tim Gaud,*" replied the operator.

Absolutely dumbfounded, Tim managed to say, "*Who?*"

Then a voice in the background cried out, "*That's him, operator! That's Pastor Tim!*"

"*Go ahead,*" came the operator's reply.

The young girl on the other end of the line was also at the end of her rope. She was contemplating suicide because, in her estimation, God had forgotten about her. In the midst of her confusion, God told her to call Pastor Tim. He assured her that she would find the help she needed.

After talking for awhile, Pastor Tim and the Lord began to mend the holes in that young girl's faith and set her back on the pathway of hope. When the conversation began to wind down, Tim asked her, "*How did you manage to get in touch with me?*"

She said, "*You are in your office in Tacoma, aren't you?*"

Tim replied, "*No, honey, I'm at a pay phone in Ohio... two thousand miles away. How in the world did you get this number?*"

"*Well,*" she said, "*when God told me to call you, He began giving me these numbers. I just got a pencil and began writing them down. When you answered the phone, I assumed this was your Tacoma office.*"

That phone call changed Tim's life and that of his family. He ran back to the restaurant with tears in his eyes crying, "*Honey, God has not forgotten us. He still knows our number.*" (source unknown).

Ever felt like God has forgotten you? That everything bad that can happen has? That there is nowhere to go and nowhere to turn? Beloved, keep your chin up! God has not forgotten you. He still knows *your* number, too! Keep your ears open for what He wants to say to you. When He speaks, your life will never be the same.

I don't know about you, but I'll never walk by another pay phone and turn a deaf ear!

74

Therefore let us stop passing judgment on one another. Instead, make up your mind not to put any stumbling block or obstacle in your brother's way.

---Romans 14:13

A lady in a faded gingham dress and her husband, dressed in a homespun threadbare suit, stepped off the train in Boston and walked timidly without an appointment into the Harvard University President's outer office. The secretary could tell in a moment that such backwoods country hicks had no business at Harvard and probably didn't even deserve to be in Cambridge. She frowned.

"We want to see the President," the man said softly.
"He'll be busy all day," the secretary snapped.
"We'll wait," the lady replied.

For hours the secretary ignored them, hoping that the couple would finally become discouraged and go away. They did not. She grew frustrated and at long last decided to disturb the President even though it was a chore she always regretted. *"Maybe if they see you for a few minutes they will leave,"* she told him.

He sighed in exasperation and nodded. Someone of his importance obviously did not have the time to spend with them, but he detested gingham dresses and homespun suits cluttering up his outer office. The President, stern-faced with dignity, strutted toward the couple. The lady spoke first. *"We had a son who attended Harvard for one year. He loved Harvard. He was happy here. But about a year ago, he was killed in a tragic accident. My husband and I would like to erect a memorial to him somewhere on campus."*

The President was not touched. He was shocked. *"Madam, we can't put up a statue for every person who attended Harvard and died. If we did, this place would look like a cemetery."*

"Oh, no," the lady quickly explained. *"We don't want to erect a statue. We thought we would like to give a building to Harvard."*

The President rolled his eyes. He glanced at the gingham dress and the homespun suit and then exclaimed, *"A building! Do you have any earthly idea how much a building costs? We have over seven and a half million dollars in the physical plant at Harvard."*

For a moment the lady was silent. The President was delighted that he had disposed of this nuisance at last. The lady turned to her husband and said quietly, *"Is that all it costs to start a university? Why don't we just start our own?"*

Her husband nodded in agreement. The President's face wilted in confusion and bewilderment as Mr. and Mrs.

Leland Stanford walked out of his office and traveled to Palo Alto, California where they established the university that bears their name in honor of a son for whom Harvard no longer cared. (Reprinted from <u>The Encourager</u>, vol. 3, issue 10, October, 1998).

Jesus was no respecter of persons. He treated everyone with dignity and respect because they were all made in the image of God. How sad that many who claim to know Him, the righteous Judge, judge others while He who has the right to judge, judges not.

Malcom Forbes said it quite well: *"You can easily judge the character of others by how they treat those who can do nothing for them or to them."* The Apostle Paul put it succinctly as well: ***"Therefore judge nothing before the appointed time; wait till the Lord comes. He will bring to light what is hidden in darkness and will expose the motives of men's hearts. At that time each will receive his praise from God"*** (I Corinthians 4:5).

Beloved, why do we judge one another? Jesus is the righteous Judge. He alone has the right to judge. Instead, let us love one another, accept one another, encourage one another. You never can tell. God may send a despicable character into your life to build a university for you. If not, why not build a memorial with your life to the One Who died tragically on a tree for you. You have enough riches in Him to do it. Maybe you could call it the University of Grace. Has a nice ring to it, doesn't it?

75

Give thanks in all circumstances, for this is God's will for you in Christ Jesus.

---I Thessalonians 5:18

Remember Ernest Maley, the poor old ditch digger? You know, the one who cut his finger off one afternoon while pouring concrete and praised God for the wad of MacDonald's napkins in the seat of his truck. God used Ernest to change my life and my attitude... forever. When I first met Ernest, he just glowed with the glory and love of God. At that time, I was pessimistic and more than a little miffed about my lot in life. I asked God what Ernest had that I didn't. God politely said, **"Me! Ernest has Me!"**

I asked the Lord to explain. Don't ever ask the Lord to explain anything unless you really want to know. Father God said... **"Kenny, the difference between you and Ernest is this: Ernest takes me *seriously*. You just take Me *literally*. You quote, 'Do not worry.' Ernest trusts Me."**

God broke my heart. I was griping and complaining over spilled milk. Ernest was praising God that he had cut off his finger. I told Father that I wanted Him to be as real to me as He was to Ernest. Father said, **"Take Me seriously. Be a doer of My Word and not a hearer only. Be radically**

189

obedient, and I will be more real to you than you can imagine."

I promised Father God that night that I would do just that. I did and my life has never been the same. He has kept His end of the bargain. He is so real to me now that I can almost reach out and touch Him. Don't misunderstand. I still have my moments. I still have doubts, fears, and frustrations, but I get over them a lot more quickly now. Life is so much better when we take Him seriously and do what He says.

I remembered Ernest not long ago. My Bride and I took a trip to Birmingham, Alabama to pick up my Baby Girl at college. As we took the exit to her school, the car just quit. I mean she died in her tracks. Test time! Gripe, complain, sing the blues, *or* give thanks in all circumstances including dead cars. I'll have to admit, my lower nature voted for the former, but my commitment to Father won out. I thought to myself, *"God is up to something good here. I don't know what it is, but all things work together for good to them who take Him seriously."*

We pulled the car off the road and called Kia to pick us up. As she arrived, I tried to start the car again. Faith, huh? Well, she cranked right up and we drove on to the college and packed up Kia's stuff. By then it was 3:30 p.m., and we did not know a soul who repairs cars in Birmingham. So, we laid hands on that car and prayed over her. We hopped in and started back home.

About thirty miles out of Birmingham, she gave up the ghost. This time, there was no pulse. We had planned to be back home by nightfall, but that plan was dead, too. I knew God was up to something.

We talked to a lady who recommended a shop in Pell City. We took Kia's car and drove into town to check it out. Dixie Auto Parts was the place. There was a sign out front

190

that said, *"Jesus is Lord!"* Inside the store, the radio was tuned to a Christian station and gospel music filled the air. Harold, the parts manager, greeted us. He was a good Christian man whom God had placed there to help us. Harold explained that the mechanic was booked up solid the next day, but that he would take care of us. By lunch the next day, the car was repaired, and we were headed home. Praise the Lord!

On the drive back home, the Lord revealed to me what He was doing. **"Kenny, that fuel pump should have quit weeks ago, but I kept it going until you reached Birmingham. Had that pump gone out on a lonely stretch of interstate, terrible things could have happened to you. Besides, you needed the rest. It was good for you, Wanda, and Kia to get a good night's sleep. You had a tough week ahead of you. Can you imagine what could have happened had the car broken down in rush hour traffic in downtown Atlanta? You and your family are precious to Me. I'm always watching over you, caring for you, loving you. Don't be afraid. Don't worry. I am always as close as the mention of My Name. And I have it all under control."**

God is good, isn't He? Doesn't it boggle your mind to think how awesome and sovereign He is? One day, God sent Ernest Maley into my life in preparation for a worn-out fuel pump in Pell City, Alabama. If he cares enough about us to individually number the hairs of our heads, then worn-out fuel pumps are nothing for Him.

Relax today and enjoy the trip. It won't be long before we're finally Home!

76

In the same way, faith by itself, if it is not accompanied by action, is dead.

—James 2:17

Adaredevil by the name of Blondin came into a small western town one day claiming that he could walk a tightrope across the local canyon. People flocked from miles around to see this fool-hearty fellow sneer in the face of death. As he stood poised and ready at the edge of the canyon, he addressed the crowd: *"Do you believe I can walk across this canyon and back on a thin thread of wire?"*

"Yes! Yes! Do it, Blondin!" And they chanted, *"Blondin! Blondin! Blondin!..."*

The crowd watched breathlessly as Blondin slid the first foot upon the wire and began his perilous journey. Minutes later he stepped triumphantly back to safety. The crowd went wild. But there was more to this show.

When the cheers subsided, Blondin again shouted to the crowd: *"Do you believe I can push a wheelbarrow across this canyon on a thin thread of wire?"*

"Yes! Yes! Do it, Blondin!" And they began to chant once again, *"Bondin! Blondin!...."*

Blondin carefully guided the front wheel of that wheelbarrow onto the wire and embarked once more upon his trip of some one hundred yards. Upon his return, even the skeptics cheered, totally convinced of this hero's prowess and ability. It was a great show, but there was still more to come.

Blondin yelled over the tumult, "*Do you believe that I can push this wheelbarrow across again...this time with a man in it?*"

Having been thoroughly convinced of this man's skill and ability, they cried, "*Yes! Do it, Blondin!*" And they cheered louder than ever.

Then Blondin said, "*Who would like to be the first to volunteer to ride across in the wheelbarrow?*" There was total silence. You could have heard a pin drop. Everyone believed he could, but they didn't believe enough to bet their own life on it. They loved to sit back and watch someone else take the risk, but no one had that much faith when it came right down to it.

Are we much different from that crowd who watched Blondin defy death walking across a canyon? Do we not say, "*Yes, Jesus, we believe you can do it!*" We watch Him perform His Word in so many miraculous ways, and we trust Him... to a point. One day, He comes to us and asks, "**Do you trust Me enough to get into My wheelbarrow? Do you trust Me enough to put your life totally into My hands... sink or swim... live or die?**"

What is your answer? The thrill and excitement of being a child of God lies in participating with Jesus, not watching from the sidelines. Why don't you hop into His wheelbarrow today? Christianity was never meant to be a "spectator sport!"

77

For everyone who has will be given more, and he will have an abundance. Whoever does not have, even what he has will be taken from him.

---Matthew 25:21

Martha Berry was the founder of the Berry School for needy children at Mount Berry, Georgia. In 1932 she was named one of the 12 outstanding women in America. She once asked Henry Ford for $1 million to assist her school. Ford coolly gave her a dime instead. She graciously accepted the dime and bought some peanuts for her schoolboys to plant. She took all the peanuts harvested that year and planted a larger field. Eventually, she sold enough peanuts to buy a piano for her music students.

Martha wrote a letter to Henry Ford thanking him for the dime and relating all that the dime had done. Ford was deeply moved and invited her to Detroit where he gave her the $1 million she originally requested.

Could it be that God wants us to faithfully use the dimes we have rather than sulking over the dollars we do not have? Look around. God never expects us to do more than we are capable of doing or give more than we have. He does expect us to be faithful in the small things.

I recall a well-respected business man who was

reduced to selling pencils on the street due to some unwise business decisions. The man not only lost his business, but his family, friends and self-respect as well. One day a store owner passed him on the street and tossed fifty cents into the beggar's hat and walked on by. Suddenly, the man stopped, turned around and said, *"Sir, I would like my pencils. I apologize to you. I mistook you for a beggar, when in actuality you are a businessman."*

The man received his pencils and went on his way. Several years later, a stranger came into the man's store. The stranger was well-dressed with a confident air about him. The stranger introduced himself and began his story.

"I want to thank you, Sir. Several years ago you bought some pencils from me outside here on the street. You told me that I was not a beggar, but a businessman. I had lost sight of that after years of disappointment. You gave back to me the self-respect I needed to get up off the street and put my life back together. I now have my family, my business and my sanity once again. Thank you for reminding me of who I was and who I am. God bless you, Sir."

Suppose that store owner had kept four bits of encouragement in his pocket. Where would that poor beggar be today? It may have been a little thing to the store owner, but not to the downtrodden businessman. We need to be reminded that big things consists of little things put together. We are all a lot wealthier than we think.

Jesus said, **"Well done, good and faithful servant! You have been faithful with a few things; I will put you in charge of many things. Come and share your master's happiness!"** (Matthew 25:21). Maybe we need to spend more time working with the dimes and quarters we have rather than complaining about the dollars we need. Faithfulness in the small things is its own reward.

Like they say when answering the pay phone at Joe's pool hall, *"Go ahead... it's your dime!"* Spend yours wisely.

78

Come unto Me, all you who are weary and burdened, and I will give you rest.

---Matthew 11:28

We have a new member at Grace Fellowship. She is about a foot and a half tall with long blonde hair. She showed up Saturday at the Ladies Luncheon. She fits in real well here. She came hungry, abused by the world and the devil, and starving for love and acceptance. Her name is *"Gracie."* Fitting, don't you think?

For those of you thinking that *Shorty* would have been a better name, let me explain. *Gracie* is a dog. A stray dog. An abused dog. Down on her luck. Rejected and beaten by people whom she loved, trusted and had high expectations.

She would come right up to Wanda, but would have nothing to do with me. I suppose that she had been treated very badly by cruel men in her lifetime. My heart went out to her the moment I saw her.

I would crouch down and call to her, *"Come on, Gracie. Come on, girl."* She would slowly sneak up and smell my outreached hand but would dart off whenever I reached

196

for her. Then she would come back. You could see the "want to" in her eyes, but the "better not" kept taking over.

Eventually, I was able to pat her on the nose... then on the head... then with both hands. I scratched her ears until the warmth of my love and acceptance overwhelmed her fear, and she submitted. She rolled over on her back and said with her big brown eyes, *"Rub me all over, please!"*

While I scratched her belly, she lay there in ecstasy. I wondered if God ever felt the way I was feeling. I was frustrated that Gracie could not see how much I wanted to touch her. How much I wanted to get my hands on her and pat her. Take care of her. Love her. Minister to her. But she could not overcome the memories of the past. The fear. The pain. The heartache.

There are so many Gracie's out there. Abused. Hurting. Rejected. Alone. Hungry. All God wants to do is love them. Forgive them. Accept them. Heal them. Touch them. But they are so afraid. Sometime. Somewhere. Someone who was supposed to be trusted betrayed them. Failed them. Abused them. All of a sudden the ground beneath their feet became sinking sand. Fear. Insecurity. Doubt. Confusion. The weeds of a faulty belief system began to grow in the potting soil of self-pity until the Truth was choked out.

When God showed up (and He was there all the time), reaching out His hand of love, mercy, grace and forgiveness, they recoiled in fear. Their hearts longed to surrender to Him, but their pain was too intense and their memories too ingrained. Nevertheless, God never stopped reaching. Begging. Pleading. Watching. Waiting.

You may be like Gracie today. God's hand is reaching for you right now. He's been through pain, too. Rejection. Betrayal. Abuse. Despair. That's why He will never give up on you. You cannot fall so far that God's grace cannot reach you.

You know you want to. Go ahead. Sniff His hand of mercy. Love. Grace. Peace. Smell the aroma? Feel the gentleness of His touch upon your nose? Move a little closer. Feels good, doesn't it? Go ahead. Take the plunge. Fall into His arms. They have been there right underneath you all the time. Longing. Waiting. Reaching. Trust him. It sure beats the alternative.

79

And the LORD asked me, "What do you see, Amos?" "A plumb line," I replied. Then the Lord said, "Look, I am setting a plumb line among my people Israel; I will spare them no longer."

---Amos 7:8

One day, a friend of mine showed me a remarkable instrument... a hand-held transit used to survey the slope of the land. The instrument looks like a small telescope. As you look through it, there appears a horizontal cross hair on the right side of the lens and a little bubble on the left that serves to show when the instrument is level. You pick out an object on the horizon and sight it through the scope. When the bubble and the cross hairs are in line, you pick a spot on a tree, or a rock, or whatever you are sighting where the cross hairs intersect. By measuring the distance from the ground up to that spot, you can determine the slope of the land. Neat!

Having experimented with the scope for a while, I began to realize that my naked eye was usually deceived. I could not believe how far off I estimated some measurements due to optical illusions. Then God began to show me that we have "spiritual" illusions as well. Because of sin and unbelief, we have a propensity to see things differently than they really are. We look through the lens of our own biases...our own interests... our own prejudices. Consequently, our perceptions of people, things, and circumstances may not really be what they appear.

If we are getting distorted messages, how do we gain a proper perspective? By looking through God's Transit... His Holy Word. The Bible shows us how things really are. We all *"fall short of the glory of God"* (Romans 3:23). *"There is, therefore now no condemnation to them who are in Christ Jesus"* (Romans 8:1). *"Love one another"* (John 13:34). *"Forgive one another"* (Ephesian 4:32)... etc.

How do I react when people treat me harshly? Without the Transit, I want to lash out. The Transit says, *"Love your enemies"* (Mathtew 5:44). *"Vengeance is mine, I will repay," says the Lord* (Romans 4:19).

How much do I need to pray? Without the Transit, I think that saying grace, or praying when I need something, is sufficient. The Transit says, *"Pray without ceasing"* (I Thessalonians 5:17).

Can you imagine laying a foundation for a house using the naked eye to make sure it's level? There would be some mighty crooked houses. There are some mighty crooked people spiritually because their lives are built upon foundations that are not surveyed with God's Transit. Sometimes it seems as if life is an uphill battle. At other times, it seems like things are going downhill. But not to worry... simply line up the bubble (you) with God's cross hair (the Bible), and you'll be surprised how quickly things will *"level out."*

80

"The tongue has the power of life and death, and those who love it will eat its fruit."

---Proverbs 18:31

I bet you didn't realize that you have a lethal weapon in your mouth. That is what God says. He, most of all, knows the power of the spoken word. He spoke the Word and all the worlds came into order. He waved His hand and planets filled the empty sky.

Do something for me right now, will you? Think back to a time when someone said something really nice to you that just blessed your heart. Go ahead. I'll wait.

Did you come up with one? How did it make you feel? I'll bet it made you feel good just thinking about it even though those words might have been spoken years ago. Am I right? I thought so.

Now think about something that was said to you that reached right into your chest and tore your heart out. Something that discouraged you or made you angry, sad, etc. I know that you don't like to think about those kinds of things, but just bear with me a minute.

When you thought about those words, it was almost as if it was happening all over again, right? You still remember it vividly. That parcel of memory, whether you admit it or not, is still affecting your life and attitude today. The spoken word has great power just like God said.

Romans 10:9-10 says... ***"That if you confess with your mouth, "Jesus is Lord," and believe in your heart that God raised him from the dead, you will be saved. For it is with your heart that you believe and are justified, and <u>it is with your mouth that you confess and are saved</u>.***

"Saved" means more than going to heaven when we die. Jesus came to save us from our sins. That means saving us from the defilement and destruction of sin. He wants us to live in joy and peace... not sorrow and confusion.

Do you see how important confessing the truth is? *Confess* in the Greek is "homologeo." It means "to say the same thing." To confess God's truth, His Word, means that we agree with what God says. When we confess anything that does not agree with God, we are agreeing with the adversary, the devil. You do not want to get in agreement with the devil. Watch what you say!

In Mark 11:22, Jesus says... ***"I tell you the truth, if anyone says to this mountain, 'Go, throw yourself into the sea,' and does not doubt in his heart but believes that <u>what he says</u> will happen, it will be done for him."*** Is that power, or what!?! If what you say can move mountains, then that little tongue has some more potential.

Do you have a mountain in your life that is blocking your view of Jesus? Ever felt like you could make it if only you could look Jesus in the face? Well, you can. You just have faith in God. Speak the Truth to that mountain, and it must move out of the way.

What's *your* mountain? A lost relationship? Sickness? Finances? Depression? Discouragement? You may not even know the name of the mountain that is causing you so much grief. Ask the Holy Spirit to identify *your* mountain. When the Lord identifies your problem, speak to it and command it to leave.

Here's one way to do that: Confess Romans 6:1ff and substitute your mountain for the word *sin*. Let's use discouragement as an example... ***"What shall I say then? Shall I continue to be discouraged that grace may abound? God forbid! How shall I that am dead to discouragement live any longer therein."***

Don't tell God about your mountain. Tell your mountain about your God. As you confess the Truth, that old mountain will come down. I guarantee it on the authority of God's Word. Keep those bulldozers of confession up and running. Put on your helmet of salvation and watch out for falling rock!

81

If anyone would come after Me, he must deny himself and take up his cross daily and follow Me.

--- Luke 9:23

There once was a young man who was very much in love with his sweetheart. He told her that he would climb Mount Everest in gym shorts and street shoes just to hold her hand. He would swim shark-infested oceans. He would even drive in rush hour traffic in downtown Charlotte.

She asked, *"Honey, are you coming over tomorrow night?"*

"I will if it doesn't rain. I just had my car waxed."

We laugh about the difference between his "talk" and his "walk." But before we go thinking what a hypocrite he is, think about what we sing and say in a worship service on Sunday. Are we practicing what we hear preached?

Is Jesus our "all in all"? Is He alone our heart's desire? Is He more precious than silver and more beautiful than diamonds? If not, then why not? Maybe it is because we have too many options available to us. We are too self-sufficient. We believe that we do our part and He fills in the gaps. No. That's not right. Jesus must be our "all in all." Without Him we can do nothing! Absolutely nothing. If we would ever come to the place where we really believed that,

203

then our walk would begin to match our talk, and the world would begin to see Jesus.

I'd like to share a letter with you from a martyred young African pastor in Zimbabwe who really believed that Jesus was his "all in all" (author unknown).

"I am part of the fellowship of the unashamed. I have Holy Spirit power. The die has been cast. I have stepped over the line. The decision has been made---I am a disciple of His. I won't look back, let up, slow down, back away, or be still. My past is redeemed, my present makes sense, my future is secure. I'm finished and done with low living, sight walking, smooth knees, colorless dreams, tamed visions, worldly talking, cheap giving, and dwarfed goals. I no longer need preeminence, prosperity, position, promotions, plaudits, and popularity. I don't have to be right, first, tops, recognized, praised, regarded, or rewarded. I now live by faith, lean on His presence, walk by patience, am uplifted by prayer, and labor with power. My face is set, my gait is fast, my goal is heaven, my road is narrow, my way rough, my companions few, my Guide reliable, my mission clear. I cannot be bought, compromised, detoured, lured away, turned back, deluded, or delayed. I will not flinch in the face of sacrifice, hesitate in the presence of the enemy, pander at the pool of popularity, or meander in the maze of mediocrity. I won't give up, shut up, or let up, until I have stayed up, stored up, prayed up, paid up, and preached up for the cause of Christ. I am a disciple of Jesus. I must go till He comes, give til I drop, preach til all know, and work til He stops me. And, when He comes for His own, he will have no problem recognizing me... my banner will be clear."

May his tribe increase!

82

Let us not become weary in doing good, for at the proper time we will reap a harvest if we do not give up.

---Galatians 6:9

A Northern Pike was caught and placed in a large aquarium for observation. Big, juicy minnows were placed in the tank with the big Pike. He thought he had died and gone to fish heaven. There was an overflowing supply of minnows and nothing to do but gobble them up... or so he thought.

Scientists put a large glass cylinder in the middle of the tank and put the minnows inside of the cylinder. The Pike could see the minnows swimming around and would dart toward one for a quick snack. Bang! His snout would flatten against the sides of the cylinder. Dazed, but persistent, he would try again and again with the same results.

Now this was a stubborn fish. Bless his heart, he bloodied his nose all day long until he finally admitted defeat. As we all know, even superlative confidence will deteriorate in the face of constant failure. Finally, he tucked his tail and settled in a corner of the tank to pout with an icebag on his nose.

The scientists then removed the cylinder and released the minnows. The minnows swam right in front of the Pike, but he didn't even flinch. He had given up on ever enjoying a "minner dinner" again.

I talk to "Pike" Christians almost everyday. They were once all excited when they first plunged into the tank of God's salvation and love. But after banging their nose against the cylinder of disillusionment for a while, they gave up on their pursuit of the "abundant life." They saw in their spirit the blessedness of the Promised Land, but all they ever got was the agony of defeat and a bloody nose to boot. Now they sit in church (if they are still in church) and lick their wounds when no one is looking and smile when people are watching. Oh, how miserable they are.

What is the problem with these "Pike" Christians? The answer is found in Hebrews 4:1-2... ***"Therefore, since the promise of entering His rest (abundant life) still stands, let us be careful that none of you be found to have fallen short of it. For we also have had the gospel preached to us, just as they did; but the message they heard was of no value to them, because those who heard did not combine it with faith."***

What's that you say? You have faith? If you had biblical faith, then there would be no glass cylinder of unbelief keeping you from your "minner dinner"... the Bread of Life.

What is biblical faith, anyway? I'm glad you asked. Faith is simply knowing the mind of God and then being obedient. It is believing something is so, even though it's not so, so it can be so, because God says it is so. Faith is acting on the Word of God as if it already is, even though it's not, so it can be, because God said it was.

Do you remember the ten lepers that Jesus healed in

206

Luke 17:11-19? He told them to go tell the priests about their healing. When they looked at their skin, they were not healed. But as they started on their way, *they were healed as they went.* Can you see that faith acts on what it believes? It doesn't sit back and wait for things to happen. Biblical faith is active, not passive. It steps out and trusts that what God says is true.

Maybe you have asked God to do something for you, but He didn't do exactly what you wanted. Maybe you asked for something that God knew would not be in your best interest. Maybe it was something good, but God wanted to give you something better. Or maybe it was not in God's timing to release it to you.

All I know is that God is good... all the time. He is perfect love and would never do anything that's not for your own good. He is perfectly wise and can never make a mistake. He is all-powerful and nothing can thwart His plans for you.

Jesus said that He came that we might have life and have it more abundantly (John 10:10). Do you believe that? Then why are you standing there? Act on it. Accept His grace and walk in His faithfulness.

Had that Pike not given up so quickly, he would still be munching minnows. Don't you make the same mistake. If the gates of hell cannot prevail against God's faithful, a little glass cylinder of unbelief doesn't stand a chance!

83

He who stands firm to the end will be saved.

---Matthew 10:22

One day, a man noticed a cocoon on his window seal. He was fascinated by this miracle of nature. As the days went by, he eagerly anticipated the marvelous appearing of a beautiful butterfly.

Finally, the long wait was over. The cocoon began to crack and one wrinkled wing emerged from the crusty shell. The man watched anxiously as the butterfly struggled intensely to free itself. Having the gift of mercy... and impatience... the man could stand the wait no longer. He could not bear watching the seemingly helpless creature struggle so. Impatience displaced wisdom. He began to help the butterfly escape by peeling away the layers of the cocoon.

At last, the butterfly was free. It lay there twitching and writhing. It's wings were wet, wrinkled and weak. Desperately the butterfly tried in vain to fly away, but to no avail. After an hour or so, the butterfly died. It had no strength to survive its environment. Its wings were too weak to lift it to the lofty heights for which it was destined.

The man did not realize that God had designed the cocoon in such a way that the butterfly would gain needed strength for life through its struggle to escape. When the man meddled with God's divine plan, the butterfly emerged into a hostile environment with no strength to meet its harsh demands. We often make the same mistake with those we love. Because of our intense love for them, we unintentionally mess with God's plan for their lives and end up thrusting them into the world unprepared to meet its challenges.

As parents, it is tough to watch our children struggle with the growing pains of life. As spiritual leaders of our homes and churches, it is difficult to keep from trying "to fix" people so they won't have to traverse some of the wilderness we've had to endure. But we must remember this: God allows the struggles so that we can become strong. The struggles force us to depend upon Him for our strength.

Acts 14:22 says..."***We must go through many hardships to enter the Kingdom of God.***" The Kingdom of God is simply anywhere that God rules and reigns absolutely. Do you see the connection? We will never allow God to have that reign in our lives unless He allows us to struggle, and we see the futility of living in our own energy and resources. Then, and only then, will we come to know that *"without Him, we can do nothing"* (John 15:5)... but *we can do all things through Him Who strengthens us"* (Philippians 4:13).

Be encouraged, Beloved. Father God knows how tough it is to be a parent and watch your kid endure the wilderness. He had a Kid, too.

84

Do not be deceived: God cannot be mocked. A man reaps what he sows.

—Galatians 6:7

In Italy, the mandatory seatbelt law went into effect on April 27, 1989. Claudio Ciaravolo, a psychiatrist in Naples, invented a "security shirt." The white T-shirt was printed with a diagonal black stripe designed to deceive the police into believing the motorist was buckled up. How interesting! I wonder if they ever had a wreck, would they be able to deceive the doctor into believing they were not hurt and bleeding?

There's an analogy here worth noting. Many people use religion to deceive others into believing that they are disciples of Christ. They may act the same as disciples... read the Bible... go to church... give their money... act religious. But the real proof of their profession is evidenced when they have a wreck in life. Jesus said, ***"In the world, you shall have tribulation (wrecks), but be of good cheer...I have overcome the world"*** (John 16:33).

As we travel life's highway, we better buckle up with the seatbelt of Truth. His seatbelt will stabilize us when the forces of tough times tug and pull at us like the centripetal forces upon an automobile. Though we may suffer some

210

minor bumps and bruises when we do have a wreck, we'll make it Home safely. Just keep your eyes on the road and buckle up, Beloved. Enjoy the trip!

85

No discipline seems pleasant at the time, but painful. Later on, however, it produces a harvest of righteousness and peace for those who have been trained by it. Therefore, strengthen your feeble arms and weak knees.

---Hebrews 12:11-12

God has a lot to teach us if we will just look around and take notice. The animal kingdom has many great object lessons which are very beneficial as we journey through the wilderness. For instance, when a baby giraffe is born, he falls ten feet and lands flat on his back. After catching his breath, he sees this gigantic, long-necked Mama hovering over him. About the time he shakes the cobwebs from his little head, Mama kicks him about ten yards across the plain. He staggers to get up... his wobbly legs weakly trying to keep him standing. Then...WHAM! She kicks him again.

I don't know about you, but that seems a rather cruel way to welcome your newborn into the world. However, mama giraffe sees it as an act of love. Her mama kicked her the same way. In the wilderness, predators abound ever ready to pounce upon the weak and wobbly. Mama knows that if he doesn't get up and strengthen those legs real quick, he will end up being a fast food entree.

Father God loves you enough to kick you around so that you can stand against the "wiles of the devil?" God knows that the devil is like a *"roaring lion seeking whom he may devour."* That's why God allows some hard knocks and kicks to our spiritual mid-sections.

Have you been a little bitter and resentful lately for some of the trials that God has allowed to come your way? Do you see them any differently after this little nature lesson? If so, why don't you take a minute to thank Him for the kicks. They may hurt for awhile, but it sure beats ending up on a short order menu at the devil's drive-thru.

86

A friend loves at all times.

—Proverbs 17:17

Ever wonder why a dog is man's best friend? Wouldn't you like to have a few Christian friends who would treat you like your dog?

Blackie has taught me much about true friendship. The way friendship ought to be. The kind of friendship we have with our Friend, Jesus, **"Who sticks closer than a brother"** (Proverbs 18:24). It does not matter what time of day or night I meet Blackie. She is always smiling and wagging her tail. Do you have any friends who are never in a bad mood?

It does not matter to her how I treat her or what kind of mood I'm in when I come home. I still get that same old slobbery kiss and excited welcome time after time. All she asks of me is a kind word and a love pat on the head. Even if I don't have time for her, she always has time for me. Do you have any friends that will keep loving you like that even in the face of neglect and indifference?

It does not matter if I forget to feed her. She will still lick my hand whether it has food in it or not. Do you have any friends who still love you when you fail to meet their needs?

It does not matter if I'm a pauper or a prince. She loves me just the same. Do you have any friends who will stand by you in the valley as well as on the mountaintop?

It matters not what foe enters our domain. She is willing to lay down her life to protect our family. She was almost shot by a policeman who came into our yard before dawn one morning. It didn't matter to her. She was protecting our home. Do you have any friends who would lay down their lives for you and your family?

I have heard of dogs literally grieving themselves to death over the loss of their master. Do you have any friends whose life is that enmeshed with yours?

When I see Blackie, I am reminded of my dearest Friend... my Lord Jesus. Blackie reminds me that Jesus loves me when I don't have time to love Him... when I take Him for granted... when I get bogged down in the day-to-day grind of life. Jesus is always there to love me... care for me... protect me... lay down His life for me.

Blackie treats me a lot better than I deserve. So does Jesus! Let's follow their example and start treating one another like a dog!

87

And the Lord blessed the latter days of Job more than his beginning.

---Job 42:12

I love happy endings, don't you? I would like to bring to a close the saga of Blackie, the most famous stray dog in our county. Hers is a story of God's grace as much as Job's and every bit as happy an ending.

Thanks to the overwhelming generosity of our church family, we were able to have Blackie spayed and inoculated. We prayed fervently for a good home. She deserved it. She's been abused, abandoned, mistreated and called to bear pups during a blizzard without food and shelter. She's lived a hard life.

I remember when we went to the pound to pick her up. Her limp tail began to wag wildly and her lonely eyes sparkled with the glint of hope. She hopped up into the car and sat there panting as happy as possum eating briars just to be in the presence of those who loved her.

One day a lady who lives out in the country saw our

ad in the paper about Blackie. This lady had lost her black Labrador Retriever with a red collar. She related to me how very much she missed her dog and had been praying for his return, or to find another dog like him. She couldn't believe it when she came to see Blackie and saw her red collar. It was a match made in heaven. She and Blackie hit it off right away.

She called me one night to tell me how well Blackie was doing and how much she appreciated all that we had done. Blackie loves her new home. She particularly likes having her stomach scratched by a master who pets rather than pounds.

We have a lot in common with Blackie, don't we? We, too, have been abused by the "accuser of the brethren"...chained and beaten with sin... lonely and hopeless... starving for acceptance and encouragement. But one day, Jesus came to pick us up at a pound called Calvary. When we saw Him, our eyes began to sparkle with hope and a new day dawned for us. And just like Blackie, we, too, will live happily ever after.

_88_

What time I am afraid, I will trust in thee.

---Psalm 53:6 (KJV)

They were on their way up to Jerusalem, with Jesus leading the way. The disciples were astonished, *while those who followed were afraid.* (Mark 10:32). Dismal times... uncertain days... fear and trepidation. Not much has changed in two thousand years, has it?

Many times Jesus said to His disciples, *"Fear not."* Then one day, He set out for Jerusalem. A cross awaited Him there. He started walking ahead, and they were fearful. The future became uncertain.

The disciples were astonished. Jerusalem did not seem like the place from which to scale the heights of the Kingdom since all the Pharisees hated Jesus and wanted to kill Him. Jesus was the Lamb approaching a pack of wolves. His followers were afraid. They sensed something momentous was about to take place although they didn't understand. I've been there, too, haven't you?

It was easy to follow Jesus early on in our walk with Him. But the day comes when He pushes ahead and says, *"Follow Me."* It is at this point that many terminate their pilgrimage. Fear rises up like an ominous beast. The faint of heart turn and run.

In the beginning, we followed Him for our own benefit. Salvation. Peace. Blessings. Fellowship. Then He raised the stakes..."*Will you follow Me for My sake and for the sake of the Kingdom?*" Then He walked ahead.

Are you at a point in your life where Jesus is walking ahead, and you don't know where He is going? Maybe He is walking deeper into the wilderness, and you think the way out is in the opposite direction. Disregard the fear and follow Him. He has not given us *"a spirit of fear, but of love, power, and a sound mind"* (2 Timothy 1:7). It's natural to fear the unknown, but *"do not be afraid, little flock, for*

your Father has been pleased to give you the Kingdom"
(Luke 12:32).

Maybe being a disciple of Jesus means being afraid most of the time and never quite understanding what's going on.... and following anyway.

89

Wherefore let him that thinks he stands take heed lest he fall.

---I Corinthians 10:12

Amy Svoboda knew better. She was a fighter pilot *par excellent*. She was chief of training for the 355th Wing's 354th Fighter Squadron at Davis-Monthan AFB. She was a 1989 graduate of the Air Force Academy. She was also the second female fighter pilot in the 355th Wing to die. All the years of training. The intensive study. The discipline. All neglected for just a matter of seconds. But that's all it took.

Capt. Svoboda was flying a routine training mission over the Arizona desert near Tucson. She dropped her four bombs and twisted her plane at a steep angle to view the impact. She was warned to check her dive angle but failed to do so. Because she failed to consult her instruments, Capt. Svoboda continued to fly upside-down while thinking all the time she was right-side up. She also felt that she was climbing when, indeed, she was diving. Her commander at

Davis-Monthan Air Force Base said, *"I am certain that Amy thought she was right-side up, because we found the engines at almost full power."*

A number of factors figured into the crash. The darkness. Impaired vision from the glare of the bombs. The "routiness" of the mission. Negligence. Misplaced trust in feelings.

Capt. Amy Svoboda should not be dead today. She knew better. Even though her occupation was hazardous, she had all the technological advantages to keep her safe. She was only negligent for about 4 to 5 seconds, and her plane hit the ground nose first at over 400 miles per hour!

Saint of God, we are not unlike Capt. Svoboda. We, too, know better. We have been highly trained. We have studied to show ourselves approved unto God (II Timothy 2:15). The Holy Spirit has written the Word upon our hearts. We have been given wings with which to mount up as eagles (Isaiah 40:31). Wings called **trust** and **obey**.

However, our trust is only as good as the object in which we are trusting. That object must be reliable. For Amy, it was her training and her instruments. For us, it is the Word of God. It is much more reliable than any instrument panel in even the most sophisticated jet fighter. We must trust it and act upon it, or else we will crash and burn.

When Capt. Svoboda needed her object of trust the most... when she was in darkness and her vision was impaired... she failed to rely upon that which could have saved her life. Beloved, we must not make the same mistake.

Are you in a dark place in your life right now? Are you seeing God's plan for your life clearly at this moment? If your life is spinning out of control, you must check your instruments... the Word of God. God's ways are not our ways. We can be flying upside-down and think we are right-side up. We can think we are climbing when in reality we are in a nose-dive.

Let's do a quick flight check: Are you confused about some things in your life? Has the glare of the world dimmed your spiritual vision? Has your walk (or flight) with God become routine and hum-drum? Are you neglecting the Word of God (your instrument panel) and prayer (your communication with the tower)? Have you logged your flight plan with the tower and received the Commander's approval? Are you walking by faith, or by your feelings?

Every pilot goes through a thorough checklist before every mission. We need to do a daily check-up to make sure we are not taking our flight with the Lord for granted. You may have checked every item on your pre-flight checklist. I'm sure Capt. Svoboda did as well. However, there is one other essential to insure a successful mission... OBEDIENCE!

You can have the finest and most accurate instrument panel in the world, but you must obey what it tells you to do. Instruments don't lie. Neither does God's Word. We cannot always trust what we feel. Feelings will lie. They are called, *"lying emotions."* Amy's lied to her, and now she's lying six feet under.

Fellow warrior, the warfare is intensifying. We are not in a training mission. We are in live combat... all out war! We are in a life and death struggle with the enemy for the souls of men and women, boys and girls not the least of which is our own. We cannot afford to be derelict in our duties. We must be unconditionally faithful to our Commander-In-Chief, the Lord Jesus.

Capt. Svoboda failed to trust and obey for 4 seconds. 4 measley seconds. Not long at all... but long enough to usher her into eternity.

She was warned and trained. So are we. ***"Be self-controlled and alert. Your enemy the devil prowls around like a roaring lion looking for someone to devour"*** (I Peter 5:8). ***"Be always on the watch, and pray that you may be able to escape all that is about to happen..."***(Luke 21:36).

Amy knew better. Do you?

90

Be self-controlled and alert. Your enemy the devil prowls around like a roaring lion looking for someone to devour.

—I Peter 5:8

Eagles have always fascinated and intrigued me. Like the writer of Proverbs I have always marveled at the way of an eagle in the air. Although a swift and cunning hunter, eagles are not beyond temptation and the throes of deception.

I remember reading a story one time about how poachers capture eagles. It is a long and tedious process but highly effective. The process is very similar to the way Satan deceives and takes us captive to do his will. God often uses the animal kingdom to demonstrate spiritual truth. This one hopefully will keep you on your toes so that you avoid being duped by the poacher of your soul.

Here's how it works. The poachers spy out the eagle's favorite fishing hole. On a bank where the eagles eat their catch, the poachers build a trap... a box or net camouflaged with branches and leaves. They prop it up with a stick and tie a string to it. Then they hide back in forest and wait for the eagle to come and feed.

At first, the eagle is very skeptical about this change in his environment. He stays away for a few days and then he cautiously returns. He senses the danger, but the lure of his favorite fishing spot overrules his doubt and fear. Before long, the trap becomes a normal, non-threatening addition to the landscape. He doesn't heed God's early warning system and lets down his guard. Big mistake!

Next, the poacher puts a fresh fish on the bank at the water's edge. At first, the eagle does not even approach the fish. God instilled in the eagle an aggressive hunter mentality whereby the eagle takes great pleasure and delight in the hunt and capturing his own food. Eagles are not scavengers. They only eat fresh meat. His intuitive senses tell him that a fish on the shore is not fresh and would be better off left to the vultures. He should listen to his intuition.

Every day the poacher leaves another fresh fish on the bank. He leaves the fish every single day knowing that any lapse in his persistence would negate all his hard, patient work to that point. After several days, the eagle saunters over to the fish. He knows better. He knows that God provides food for him, but He doesn't throw it in the nest. He knows that the act of hunting keeps him strong and vibrant. But once again, he denies his intuition. He smells the fish. It's fresh. He thinks it must be a blessing from heaven. After all, it is strenuous swooping and diving for fish. And so, like Eve, he eats the forbidden food. He is hooked.

The next day, he eats the fish... and the next... and the next. Now, the poacher closes in for the capture. The eagle has become comfortable with the presence of the trap in his little world. He has become a little lazy and unobservant as he eats the fish that he no longer has to catch. Having let down his guard, the poacher now places the fish farther up the bank and closer to the trap. One day the fish is placed right underneath the trap. The eagle, now oblivious to any danger, walks right into the trap and begins eating the fish. Quickly the poacher pulls the string, and the eagle is trapped.

The eagle, the symbol of freedom, is now a jail bird. He has been taken captive by the enemy all because he did not pay attention. He failed to take God seriously. God made him in such a way as to protect him and to provide for his needs. When he took all that for granted, it was just a matter of time until he lost his freedom and became earth bound.

Satan, the great poacher of our souls, plots the same strategy for us. He sets traps for us and camouflages them with deceit, lies, and yes... even religion. We sense in our spirit that something is not quite right, but we listen to our soul rather than our Spirit. We let our guard down and accept the trap as a mere addition to our environment. Then he starts feeding us with food we don't have to catch ourselves. We come to church and expect the pastor to spoon feed us the Word of God... to tell us what to believe... how to live. We become lazy in our devotions and Bible study. We let the pastor and the prayer warriors do our praying for us.

When we let our guard down, Satan brings people into our lives who deceive us. They may appear to be an answer to prayer... sweet, good, and righteous... but they are simply the bait of the enemy. We enter into soul ties and wrong agreements with them. We bear our souls to them and become transparent. And then... WHAM! The trap is sprung, and we are jailed.

The eagle listened to his soul... his mind, will, and emotions... rather than the intuition which Father God had placed within him. It cost him his freedom. The same thing can happen to us. We live in extremely dangerous days. The world, our soul, and the devil are becoming increasingly dangerous and deceitful.

Beloved, listen to the Word of God... *"They perish because they refused to love the truth and so be saved. For this reason God sends them a powerful delusion so that they will believe the lie and so that all will be condemned who have not believed the truth but have delighted in wickedness"* (2 Thessalonians 2:10-12).

"Saved" means saved from ourselves. We are our own worst enemy. Whenever we do not love the Truth... take God seriously and act upon His Word... we will be deceived. We will lose our freedom.

Beloved, take Him seriously. Listen to the Holy Spirit as He guides and speaks to your Spirit. Be sober and vigilant. Satan, like a roaring lion, walks about patiently setting traps for you in order to poach your soul. Don't you let him. You do what that eagle should have done. Eagles were never meant to be earthbound. They were born to fly. And so were you. Keep your eyes open and your wings spread!

91

Be on your guard; stand firm in the faith; be men of courage; be strong.

--- I Corinthians 16:13

We live in a world determined to have its own way. *"If it feels good, do it."* That's the battle-cry of the world. The world's system is a turmoil of confusion and skepticism. Is there any way out of this dense fog that entraps us and blinds us to the destiny Father God has placed within us? Yes. I believe there is.

The other night I dreamed I was an eagle. I was soaring in a circular pattern and looking down on the ground below. Out of nowhere ravens began to swoop down upon me and aggravate me. I simply caught an updraft and flew so high that they could not reach me. As the winds began to blow harder and stronger, I spread my wings as wide as I could and spun rapidly up into the clouds. There, high in the sky, was such a peace. No distractions. The only sound was the rush of the wind whispering in my ears. Peace. Wonderful peace.

I have been bombarded of late with the ravens of opinion, logic and reason. The winds of adversity have turned out to be a love gift from Father. As I have stretched my wings of trust and obedience, the storm has lifted me high above the realm of the distractors.

There among the clouds, I've found the essence of true leadership. It is simply following Jesus. Putting your feet into His footprints. Simply daring to go where you have not gone before. It is a lonely climb until you reach His presence. True peace is found there. It is the only place where you can see clearly enough to lead others.

You will find that the higher you fly, the fewer there will be that follow. But that's okay. A true leader has the confidence to stand alone, the courage to make tough decisions, and the compassion to listen to the needs of others. He does not set out to be a leader, but becomes one by the quality of his actions and the integrity of his intent. In the end, leaders are like eagles. They don't flock. You find them one at a time.

92

And when the LORD sent you out from Kadesh Barnea, He said, "Go up and take possession of the land I have given you." But you rebelled against the command of the LORD your God. You did not trust him or obey him.

---Deuteronomy 9:23

When God's people came into the Land of Promise, He told them to go in and take possession of it, but they refused. They saw the giants, the strong-walled cities, and the intimidation of the enemy. They were afraid. They did not trust God, and thus would not obey Him. Trust and obey... the two wings that allow us to soar to victory over all the giants in life. Pull in your wings, and you fall like a turkey.

Psalm 56:3 says, *"What time I am afraid, I will trust in You."* When fear strikes you, do you trust God and walk in obedience to His revealed will? Are you one of those about whom the writer of Hebrews speaks when he says, *"But we are not of those who shrink back and are destroyed, but of those who believe and are saved"?* (Hebrews 10:39). Or do you shrink back and bow to fear? Fear is actually faith in the enemy.

The Bible tells us that the weapons of our warfare are not carnal, but mighty through God. We battle the enemy in the spiritual realm. If satan can get you to stand against him in the energy of the flesh, he can defeat you before the battle ever begins.

The problem facing the carnal believer is his lack of trust in God and His Word. Simply stated, he does not take God's Word seriously. Taking God at His Word is simple... just DO what He says.

If you have a problem obeying God, then you have a trust problem. You cannot believe God (trust in, rely upon, cling to, put your whole weight upon) because you don't think He is reliable. True or false? Be honest.

It's scary to trust God, because you're the one who's been in control all your life. Letting go and letting God is easier said than done. Been there... done that! However, when you get tired of beating the devil's fist with your nose, you are ready to try God's way. Let me tell you something... *God has never let me down.*

I have been *really* trusting and obeying him for several

months now. He's still faithful. I know people who have been trusting and obeying for fifty years, and He's still faithful. I know that I know that I know that He is the Faithful One. He can be trusted.

God stands like a pleading father treading water underneath the diving board waiting for his 3 year old to take his first dive off the big board. Like that earthly daddy, God would drown before He would let anything harmful come to His child. Jesus proved God's faithfulness at the cross. But unlike that earthly daddy, God is not treading water. He stands rock solid waiting to catch you as you plummet wide-eyed into His loving arms.

Isn't it interesting how that same child who took forever to get up the courage to jump off the board can't wait to get out of the water and do it again once his fear is gone and trust is established? The same is true for you, Beloved. Try Him. Test Him. Prove Him. It is not a blind leap of faith. He is there. He promises to catch you. Will you trust Him? Then prove it. Jump. Obey. Step out on His Word.

Many years ago I was fascinated by an article in a *Weekly Reader*. Remember those? On the front page was a picture of a white mouse swimming under water in an aquarium. The mouse was not swimming in water, but in a so-called "miracle solution." The solution was highly oxygen-enriched. The mouse was actually breathing the fluid instead of air. He seemed to be having a ball swimming around in that stuff. It amazed me.

Years later, a movie came out called *The Abyss*. In the movie, a nuclear bomb had been accidentally dropped in a deep, deep canyon in the ocean floor which required defusing. The canyon was so deep and narrow that conventional diving equipment was inadequate.

The hero of the movie consented to make the dive

in an unconventional diving suit filled with this oxygen-enriched solution. When they placed the glass helmet over his head and began pumping the liquid into the suit, you could see the panic in his eyes as the fluid rose above his mouth and nose. He held his breath as long as he could. When he could hold his breath no longer, he breathed the solution into his lungs. He shook violently, expecting the fluid to drown him. Instead, a calmness and a peace came over his face when he realized that he was breathing the fluid better than he had ever breathed air.

That scene is so applicable to our trusting and obeying God. There are some deep, dark places in life through which all of us must go... disappointments... illnesses... broken relationships... trials and tribulations. These places are too deep for us to survive with conventional means of coping. Fleshly attempts to deal with life's canyons lead only to panic and destruction. Only God's solution will enable us not only to survive, but to thrive at those depths.

Nonetheless, we are not used to breathing God's solution. We panic when circumstances force us to trust Him or die. We quiver and shake when the very means of our survival... the solution of trust and obedience... rise above our mouths and noses. But when we finally commit ourselves to His solution, the sweetness of His breath of Life floods over us.

The heights and the depths to which God longs to take us cannot be scaled with conventional faith. We must take God at His Word. When we do, the panic will cease and peace will fill our souls.

The devil is constantly trying to steal your joy, your peace, your destiny. For some of you, he already has. Take a deep breath of God's faithfulness and dive down to take back what rightfully belongs to you! Go ahead. You can only hold your breath for so long.

93

In Him we were also chosen, having been predestined according to the plan of Him Who works out everything in conformity with the purpose of His will.

---Ephesians 1:11

Some time ago we watched the movie, *Apollo 13.* It was, indeed, an exciting movie. It kept me on the edge of the couch until the very end. Maybe I'm the only one who notices stuff like this, but I saw the sovereignty of God so very evident in that perilous mission. For instance, one member of the original crew, the pilot of the command module, was bumped from the flight because the doctor believed that he was on the verge of breaking out with the measles. Needless to say, he was sad, mad and bitter over the death of his dream to go to the moon.

The astronaut who replaced him was not nearly as proficient as the "bumped" pilot. Everyone involved in the mission was already a little uneasy because this was Apollo **13** which was scheduled to land on the moon on April **13**, 1970.

Many never see that the sovereignty of God

supercedes superstition. God is always in control... all the time. God knew what was going to happen on that mission. He placed each and every single one of the people on that team just where He wanted them. When tragedy struck the spacecraft as they orbited the moon, the "bumped" astronaut was the only one back on earth who could get the stranded crew back home. Does God know some stuff or what!?!

What often appears to us as disappointment is simply God's appointment to something far better than we could imagine. He is so wise and so good! How foolish we are to think we know what is best for us. God sees the beginning and the end as well as the middle. All we ever see is what's going on right now.

The Lord has all the facts. He alone knows how He wants things to work out. And if He loves like He says He does, then He will not and cannot allow anything to happen that is not in accordance with His perfect love. Do you believe that? If not, you are living a miserable existence wading through the wilderness shrouded by "what if's" and "supposes." God has an answer for every "what if..." You can trust Him. He does love and care for you perfectly. Rest in that love today. He cares for you even when you get a little "spacey" and wonder if you will ever make it Home!

94

Miriam sang to them: "Sing to the Lord, for He is highly exalted. The horse and its rider He has hurled into the sea."
—Exodus 15:21

B oy, howdy! Was that something or what? God just ripped open the Red Sea and the Hebrew children walked across on dry ground. He then closed it back up with the entire Egyptian army in the middle of it. Talk about a victory! Miriam burst forth in song and praise. It was glorious, indeed. God was good! All was well!

Shortly thereafter, they entered the desert wilderness. They traveled for three days without water. Three is the number of testimony. You cannot have a testimony without a "test." Two to three million people in a desert without water... Now, I'd consider that a TEST, wouldn't you? As usual, they failed. They grumbled at Moses unmercifully. *"Where's the water? Did you bring us out here to die?"*

They finally came to Marah. There was water, but it was bitter. That was a real test. They found water... hope arose... then hope was dashed to pieces. Cruel, wasn't it? Bless Moses' heart. He is one of my Biblical heroes. Whenever my little flock begins to grumble, I think of Moses' three million gripers and smile. Thank God He didn't give me three million grumblers to lead. Moses was only doing what God told him. But God was telling him to go to some pretty unseemly places... like deserts and wilderness. I'm sure Moses thought that God has lost His road atlas.

Nevertheless, Moses knew what to do. He cried out to the Lord. The Lord showed him a piece of wood. Moses threw it into the water, and the water became sweet. Right there, the Lord laid down one of His very first lessons on wilderness survival: ***"If you listen carefully to the voice of the Lord your God and do what is right in His eyes, if you pay attention to His commands and keep all His decrees, I will not bring on you any of the diseases I brought upon the Egyptians, for I am the Lord, Who heals you"*** (Exodus 15:26).

I believe the wood that God showed Moses was symbolic of the Cross. The Cross represents death. Death to my agenda, my control, my will, my way. When I allow the Cross to do its effectual work in my life, I don't grumble. Dead people don't complain. From this account, there were three million very *alive* people wandering in the wilderness.

Beloved, there have been and will be many deserts on your journey to the promised land. There will be a lot of bitter pools from which you will have to drink. But if you always say, *"Yes, Lord,"* the Cross will sweeten those bitter pools. You will also discover that those bitter pools will not only become drinkable, they will refresh and strengthen you.

God's Word is often referred to as Water. Some of God's Word is bitter to our taste. Our tastebuds are geared to our likes and desires rather than His. But if we delight ourselves in Him, He will give us the desires of our hearts. If we seek Him first, then all the other things will be added. The secret is in the "water-sweetener"... the Cross of Christ.

Wood you let His Cross sweeten your bitter waterhole today?

232

95

"Why do you call me, 'Lord, Lord,' and do not do what I say? I will show you what he is like who comes to me and hears my words and puts them into practice. He is like a man building a house, who dug down deep and laid the foundation on rock. When a flood came, the torrent struck that house but could not shake it, because it was well built. But the one who hears my words and does not put them into practice is like a man who built a house on the ground without a foundation. The moment the torrent struck that house, it collapsed and its destruction was complete."
—Luke 6:46-49

Wilderness wanderer, we've come a long way on our journey together. I hope and pray that the waterholes along the way have helped to quench your thirst for Living Water. Thirst is good. Jesus said, ***"Blessed are those who hunger and thirst for righteousness, for they will be filled"*** (Matthew 5:6).

Father God loves you so much. He has a great plan and purpose for your life. A destiny beyond your wildest dreams. All He asks is your trust and obedience. He will do the rest. He will lead you beside still waters and restore your soul if you will only follow Him. He is the Way... the only Way out of your wilderness. Will you, right now, surrender totally to His Lordship? Will you follow Him wherever He leads? If you are ready to step into the Promised Land, then give Him your whole heart. Settle the issue once and for all. If you are ready to take Him seriously, let's pray:

Heavenly Father, You know how rebellious I have been. You know that I don't take your Word as seriously as I should. I ask Your forgiveness for my unbelief... for manipulating circumstances and people so that I can be in control rather than You... so I can get my way rather allowing You to have Your way in my life. Please forgive me for taking Your rightful place as Lord of my life. May Your will be done in me, even as it is in heaven.

Father, my life has been out of control because I have been in control. I submit myself to You. I will resist the devil, and he must flee from me.

I acknowledge that obedience is better than sacrifice. Father, You are much more interested in my listening to You than in my offering material things to You. Rebellion is as bad as witchcraft. Stubbornness is as bad as worshiping idols. Forgive me for practicing witchcraft and worshiping idols.

Heavenly Father, You deserve honesty from my heart... utter sincerity and truthfulness. Forgive me when I am not honest with You. Lord, I want to follow You. Right now, I put aside my own desires and conveniences. I yield to You my desires that are not in Your plan for me. Even in the midst of my fear, I surrender and entrust my future to You. I choose this very minute to take up my cross and follow You wherever You lead me. I will conform to Your will for me in daily living, and if need be, in dying as well.

Lord Jesus, You are my Lord. I choose to be Your servant. I am Yours and You are mine.

Heavenly Father, help me to walk through the daily process of surrendering my all to You. I exchange my rebellion and stubbornness for a willing and obedient heart. When I refuse to listen to You, anoint my ears to hear Your voice alone. When I am blinded by my own desires, open my eyes to see.

I belong to Jesus Christ, the Anointed One Who breaks down and destroys every yoke of bondage. In Jesus' Name and in obedience to Your will, Father, I submit to the control and direction of the Holy Spirit Whom You have sent to live in me. I am Your child. I am not ashamed of the Gospel. All to You I surrender. I am an overcomer by the blood of the Lamb, by the Word of God, and finally, I love You more than my own life.

Be glorified in me, Lord. Now and forever more! In Jesus' Name. AMEN!

96

I have come that they may have life, and have it to the full.
—John 10:10

P aul told Timothy to encourage people *"to put their hope in God, Who richly provides us with everything for our enjoyment"* (I Timothy 6:17). What a wonderful God and Father He is. How it must grieve His heart to see us rush by those things He has lovingly placed here for our enjoyment. We tend to worry over the seemingly urgent things of life and fail to savor those little luxuries which God surrounds us

with each day. A gentle breeze upon a sweat-soaked face...
a child's exuberant hug...a bird of prey soaring effortlessly
against a cloudless sky...a summer sunset with soft hues of
pink, orange and blue...the soothing peace of a waterfall...
the warmth of sand between your toes...the rumbling of
waves upon the beach at twilight...

The list is endless once you slow down enough to
notice them. How many memories do you have of just
taking time to soak in the goodness of God? In your haste to
get out of the wilderness, don't forget to take time to smell
the roses. Beloved, Jesus gave His Life so that we could
enjoy ours.

Let me leave you with a few "short cuts" to the
Promised Land...

- Don't postpone joy.
- Be forgiving of yourself and others.
- Always have something beautiful in sight, even if it's just a daisy in a jelly glass.
- Learn to disagree without being disagreeable.
- Don't use time or words carelessly, neither can be retrieved.
- Buy a bird feeder and hang it so that you can see it either at work or at home.
- Don't let anyone talk you out of pursuing what you know to be a great idea.
- After you've worked hard to get what you want, take time to enjoy it!

Be blessed today, Wilderness Wanderer. The
Promised Land is right around the bend!

For additional copies of this book
OR
for information about
Kenny's weekly email ministry,
The Graceline,
please contact:

Grace Fellowship Church
409 Polkville Road
P.O. Box 2404
Shelby, NC 28151
Office: (704) 484-9098
Fax #: (704) 482-7181
email: kashley@shelby.net